THE AGELESS RELICTS

BOOKS BY NORMAN TAYLOR

Taylor's Encylopedia of Gardening
Flight from Reality
Cinchona in Java
Guide to the Wild Flowers
Color in the Garden
Fragrance in the Garden
The Permanent Garden
Herbs in the Garden
The Everblooming Garden
Fruit in the Garden
Mathews' Field Book of American Wild Flowers
    (revision)
Taylor's Garden Guide
The Guide to Garden Flowers
The Ageless Relicts

"The biggest tree in the world," named for General Sherman, is in the Sequoia National Park. It is 273.9 feet high, 37.3 feet in diameter, and estimated as about 3,500 years old.

THE AGELESS RELICTS

The story of *Sequoia*

NORMAN TAYLOR

ST MARTIN'S PRESS
New York

Relict. *n.*
    2. A widow
    6. *Phytogeography.* A living remnant of an otherwise extinct type of plant, as *Sequoia,* and certain Australian cycads.
        Webster's New International Dictionary Second Edition.
Relict is used, in sense 6, throughout this book in preference to *relic.*

Copyright © 1962 by Norman Taylor
All rights reserved
Library of Congress Catalog Card Number: 62-18727
Manufactured in the United States of America
Designed by Joan Wall

PREFACE

THE IMMENSE LITERATURE on the big-tree and the redwood scarcely invites another book about them. But a century ago the impact of both trees affected the history of California, New York, and London. It is these snippets of history, intertwined with the fabulous *Sequoia*, that may furnish an excuse for this book. Scarcely anyone has linked the trees with P. T. Barnum, Horace Greeley, James Gordon Bennett, Prince Albert, Queen Victoria, Sir Joseph Paxton, and the irascible Duke of Wellington.

Such linkage is buried in the musty files of old newspapers, in many historical memoirs, and in some technical periodicals. These, plus three trips to *Sequoia*-land, prompt the hope that Californians may forgive a New Yorker for adding to the literature of *Sequoia*!

N. T.

Elmwood
Princess Anne,
Maryland

ACKNOWLEDGMENTS

AMONG THE MANY kind persons who have helped, often unconsciously, in the preparation of this book are Francis P. Farquhar, whose *Yosemite: The Big Trees and the High Sierra* is already a classic; Emanuel Fritz, whose Bibliography of California Coast Redwood, issued in 1957, is a most scholarly compilation of two thousand titles; William H. Fairbanks, Jr., Deputy State Forester, Division of Forestry; Father John B. McGloin, S.J., Archivist, University of San Francisco; Msgr. James Culleton, Director of the Academy Library Guild, Fresno; Newton B. Drury, Secretary of Save-the-Redwoods League; the late Edmund Schulman of the University of Arizona's Laboratory of Tree-Ring Research; and finally, my friend Donald Culross Peattie and his admirable *Natural History of Western Trees*. While my obligation to these gentlemen is profound, it is of course understood that none of them is responsible for any statement in this book.

CONTENTS

	Preface v
	Acknowledgments vii
one	The Big-Tree and the Gold Rush 3
two	Greed and the Big-Tree 12
three	The Big-Tree in the Sierras 25
four	Before the Dawn of History 37
five	The Redwood 55
six	The Big-Tree in New York and London 74
seven	What's in a Name? 93
eight	Where They Can Be Found 97
nine	Bibliography 105
	Index 111

THE AGELESS RELICTS

one

THE BIG-TREE
AND THE GOLD RUSH

ON FRIDAY MORNING, September 15, 1848, the *New York Tribune* announced the discovery of gold in California. It had been found by John Marshall, at Sutters Mill, Coloma, on January 24 of that year—but it took nearly eight months for the news to reach the East as it had to wait for a ship to carry it around Cape Horn.

Coloma is still a hamlet on the American River about sixty miles east and north of Sacramento, but the news came from what is now San Francisco. Then it was a miscellaneous collection of shanties clustered along the beach of the harbor, had less than a thousand people, and had only just abandoned the old Spanish name of Yerba Buena.

Within a year the gold rush had inundated this sleepy little town, and these forty-niners forever changed the history of California. But not without some penalties, for the town was soon in the throes of Vigilance Committees' attempts to curb the crimes that followed the gold rush. The city seethed with vice, corruption, and the extortionate rapacity of storekeepers, who soaked the luckless pioneers all they could stand. By 1852 thirty thousand optimistic gold seekers were reaching California annually, mostly living in tents and shanties.

So great was the lure of gold that San Francisco's superb harbor was "filled with rotting sailing vessels whose crews had deserted to go to the gold fields"; there were at one time nearly four hundred such derelict ships.

No gold, however, was to be found in San Francisco; only in the foothills of the Sierras. From one camp in those pine-clad hills, in 1852, came not only a fabulous report of gold, but amazing news of a very different sort. After more than a century the subject of the story is still one of the wonders of the world, and that story trickled down from the Sierras from a place called Murphy's Camp in Calaveras County.

The Murphy brothers, John and Dan, had taken out nearly two million dollars' worth of gold. By the spring of 1852 their fortune and name had drawn to this Sierra hillside a choice collection of miners, gamblers, prostitutes, and failures, with a fair sprinkling of Mexicans, Indians, Chinese, and bandits—notably Bill Holt.

Not long before, flour was still costing two hundred dollars a barrel and whisky twenty dollars a bottle—if you had one. But bottles were so scarce that one enthusiast, armed only with a straw, paid ten dollars for one good swig from the bung-hole. Saturday nights were usually deafening, and the five shots that ended the career of Bill Holt were scarcely noticed. The killer gave himself

The story of Sequoia

up to the Vigilance Committee and was immediately exonerated, as Holt was the most dangerous of over one hundred bandits that infested Calaveras County.

Understandably the responsible miners were already pining for the good old days of the autumn of 1848 and early 1849, when theft was unknown and gold dust was safely left in tent or cabin and even tools, literally worth their weight in gold, were left undisturbed in the diggings.

Like the Rhinegold, California's riches soon brought the inevitable curse. One of the few historians of Murphy's laments that by late 1849 "this honesty was not to be found in the . . . hordes of pickpockets, robbers, thieves, and swindlers. . . . Murders and robberies soon became the order of the day." These amenities of a gold rush camp were soon overshadowed by a very practical and much more serious difficulty, the solution of which was the cause of this book. While Murphy's Camp was an unquestioned rip-roaring success, its only flaw was the growing shortage of water of which huge quantities were needed for washing out the gold; hence the establishment of the Union Water Company by a group of affluent miners. It was an ambitious scheme, calling for the tapping of a branch of an upcountry river fifteen miles from Murphy's, and much higher in the Sierras. Using canals, ditches, sluiceways, and often bridging deep cañons, the plan demanded a large labor force, which required much food. This was still scarce and expensive.

To provide cheap food for a large working gang the company hired four good hunters to bring in game from the heavy forests. One of these was A. T. Dowd, who quite unwittingly was to make his name and Murphy's Camp known throughout the civilized world—but not for its gold.

In the spring of 1852, from Murphy's Camp in the Sierras, A. T. Dowd, in tracking down a wounded grizzly, found the big-tree in Calaveras County, but he was not the first to see it. See pages 9 and 10. (Courtesy of John Howell Books)

Soon after the discovery of the big-tree in Calaveras County the Mammoth Tree Grove became world famous. See page 11. (Courtesy of John Howell Books)

Dowd was an intrepid wanderer, for his hunting grounds practically coincided with the usual hangout of such bandits as "Three-fingered Garcia." This worthy had once robbed six Chinese and then "tied them up by their queues and cold-bloodedly cut their throats." Nothing daunted by such outrages, Dowd penetrated to the end of the company's sluiceway and even far beyond. Here, near the Stanislaus River, in southern Calaveras County, he was one day tracking down a grizzly which he had wounded.

What was his amazement—and it would have amazed far more knowledgeable observers than Dowd—to find among the dense evergreen forests *the largest tree in the world!* All thoughts of hunting were abandoned and he went back to camp full of the story of this stupendous tree. No one would believe him, and the more ribald thought he was drunk.

Smarting under this implication, he bided his time and let the jibes about his big tree die down. Then on a quiet Sunday morning he rushed into camp, after a faked "absence" of an hour or two, and announced that he had shot "the largest grizzly bear that I ever saw in my life." The grizzly was also a fake, but it was enough to get all the doubters into the woods. Dowd led them through groves of magnificent pines and firs, deep into cañons, whetting their appetite by tales of other grizzlies. Finally he reached the base of the tree and exultingly pointing to it yelled, "Now, boys, do you believe my big-tree story? That is the large "grizzly" I wanted you to see."

J. M. Hutchings, who was there, admits that this crew of rough miners were astounded and that they "stood speechless with profound awe . . . under these forest giants." The world has not yet ceased to do so, for no one who first sees

The story of Sequoia

them can ever forget the shattering impact of these monsters of the forest.

Soon after, the Sonora *Herald* published an account of Dowd's exploit, and San Francisco and English newspapers soon caught up with it.

So far as the world then knew, this spring day (it was probably in April) of 1852 saw the discovery of the first *Sequoia gigantea* ever seen by white men. Dowd had stumbled upon what is now known as the Calaveras Grove (or North Grove) to which, by the generosity of Mr. John D. Rockefeller, Jr., there has recently been added the South Calaveras Grove, just across the border in Tuolumne County. Together they comprise about 470 acres of mostly virgin stand.

But other people, before Dowd, had seen *Sequoia gigantea*. There is the persistent rumor that John Bidwell had been to the Calaveras Grove in 1841. He afterward ran for Congress from California but, leaving no records, there is nothing to support his "discovery" of the big-trees. Much more certain is the fact that starting from Murphy's Camp, two men, on May 20, 1850, discovered the grove while hunting. "Twelve days later J. Marshall Wooster, William Quirk, and one known only as Sanburn, visited the grove and carved their names on the burnt part of one of the trees." But having left no contemporary records, they are never credited with the "discovery." Nor can they be here, for they too, had a predecessor.

In 1833, an adventurous Yankee from Clearfield County, Pa., joined the expedition of F. R. Walker to go from Great Salt Lake to California. He was Zenas Leonard, who kept a journal of the trip, which was published as an 87-page book in 1839 at Clearfield, Pa. That edition is now one of the rarest of Americana. The Walker expedition is credited with having comprised the first white men to cross the Sierra Nevada from east to west. Leonard, in what must be the first printed record of *Sequoia gigantea*, wrote:

> In the last two days travelling we have found some trees of the red-wood species, incredibly large—some of which would measure from 16-18 fathoms (96-108 feet) round the trunk at the height of a man's head from the ground.

There is no other North American tree of which this is true, and Leonard saw them in what is now known as the Mariposa Grove, near Yosemite, and about fifty miles southeast of the Calaveras Grove.

Unfortunately the Leonard book was forgotten for many years, and not until its re-issue in Cleveland in 1904 did *Sequoia* historians know that Leonard was not only the discoverer of the big trees, but had published an account of it. In the meantime the world had ample proof of the Dowd discovery. It was then literally and for years the only "authentic" one. That is why Murphy's Camp was mentioned in the august chambers of the Royal Horticultural Society and in the *Times* of London, while Clearfield, Pa., was known then only as a relatively obscure town in central Pennsylvania. But from this town without much doubt came the discoverer of the most fabulous tree in the world.

Neither Leonard in 1833, nor Dowd in 1852, nor in fact did anyone else know that the Mariposa and Calaveras groves were only two of about seventy isolated groups of *Sequoia gigantea* that were subsequently found in the magical Sierra range. The trees towered above all others in the forest, but always in such dense woods and so far from any

The story of Sequoia

roads that for years no one but intrepid hunters, travelers, or botanists ever saw them.

The chief exception was the Calaveras Grove, which soon became a Mecca for the curious. As Murphy's Camp became a relatively civilized town, built a hotel of sorts, and was accessible by road, visitors from all over the world came to Murphy's as the starting place for Calaveras. Such was the fame of the trees that the Duke of Sutherland, Henry Ward Beecher, Asa Gray, Horace Greeley, President Garfield, Professor Brewer of Yale, and a host of lesser notables had visited the Calaveras Grove and many of them went also to the Mariposa Grove.

By 1870 most of the larger groves of the big-tree had been discovered. It was found that they extended from a small grove in the Tahoe National Forest, about twenty miles west of Lake Tahoe, for 260 miles southward to the huge concentration of them, and their scattered outposts, in Sequoia and Kings Canyon National Parks. All of them are on the western slopes of the Sierra Nevada, mostly at elevations of between 4000 and 7500 feet, but a few are below 4000 feet and some as high as 8900 feet in the southern part of its range. Seventy-two distinct groves are now known, nearly all of them in National or State Parks or Forests.

two

GREED AND THE BIG-TREE

Soon after the discovery of the Calaveras Grove, cupidity, charlatanism, and showmanship dominate the story of *Sequoia*. Enterprising rascals were quick to see that pictures in the *Illustrated London News*, *The Gardeners' Chronicle*, and *Gleason's Pictorial*, unbelievable as they were, and invaluable as publicity, would be completely dwarfed by actual exhibition of one of the trees.

Such an enterprising idea presented one insuperable difficulty. Any tree worth showing would have to be nearly thirty feet in diameter. Such a monster might be anywhere from 270 to 325 feet high and would, as we now know, weigh over two thousand tons. Also, the felling of it was likely to be an extremely hazardous undertaking.

There is no record that any of the vandals knew or cared

The story of Sequoia

about the utter ruthlessness of what they were determined to accomplish. But they scandalized the world and *Gleason's Pictorial* for October 1, 1853 merely reflected this horror when it stated:

> Probably it will not be very long before our readers will be able to get a view of this monster of the California woods for a trifling admission fee. In Europe such a natural production would have been cherished and protected, if necessary by law; but in this money-making, go-ahead community, 30 or 40 thousand dollars are paid for it, and the purchaser chops it down and ships it off for a shilling show.
>
> In its natural condition, rearing its majestic head towards heaven, and waving in all its native vigor, strength and verdure, it was a sight worth a pilgrimage to see; but now alas, it is only a monument to the cupidity of those who have destroyed all there was of interest connected with it.

The first great tree to be desecrated for exhibition purposes was 302 feet high and at the ground level 96 feet in circumference. The bark was stripped off for thirty feet and sold, with a cross section of the trunk, for exhibition first in San Francisco and then in New York. But felling such a monstrous tree was a problem. No saws then in use were of any avail, and the attempt to chop down such a colossus suggested impotent Lilliputians puttering about the base of a giant.

Finally a new technique was invoked. Huge augurs were used to bore holes in the trunk from the bark to as near the center as they could get. This took five men twenty-two days, but the tree refused to fall in spite of their completely ringing it with augur holes. Wedges were then inserted and driven in by huge logs hung by ropes from the trunk. Still

The scaly, juniper-like leaves and cones of the big-tree, Sequoia gigantea. (*Natural size*)

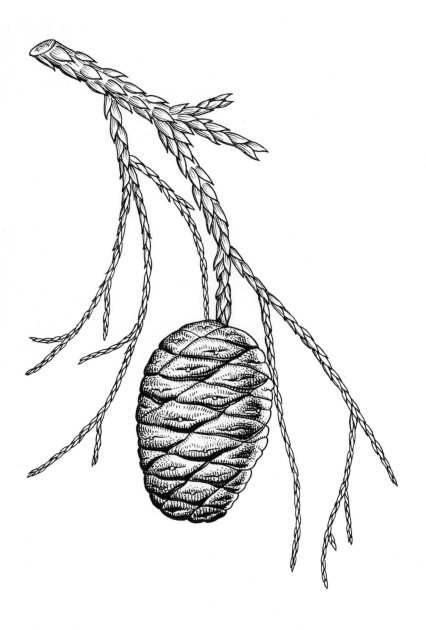

the tree stood, and all the workers and hangers-on were in the gravest danger, for no one knew when wedges or the wind would finally conquer it.

One day, when everyone was safely at lunch, a sudden gust of wind caught the monster off-balance and it crashed to the ground. No one today will ever see such a tree fall, for now over 93 per cent of all *Sequoia gigantea* is in protected groves. The earth shook as though by an earthquake for thousands of feet from the center of what one observer called "the botanical tragedy." Everything in its path was crushed, all its branches splintered to bits, and its badly shattered trunk, broken into many huge sections, was half buried in the ground.

So in the summer of 1853 was destroyed the first big-tree ever to fall by the hand of man. J. M. Hutchings, who visited the site on July 4, 1854, wrote, "However incredible it may appear . . . the writer formed one of a cotillion party of 32 persons dancing upon this stump, in addition to which the musicians and lookers-on numbered 17, making a total of 49 occupants on its surface at one time." Soon a pavilion was erected over the stump and became a trysting spot for parties from San Francisco. A hotel had already been built in the Calaveras Grove as its owners realized it would soon draw hosts of visitors. It is the nearest big-tree grove to San Francisco, which by motor is scarcely three hours away.

The staggering weight of even a few feet of the trunk, and the great difficulty of moving anything in such a mountainous country, prevented anyone from trying to exhibit a trunk with its bark on for many years. Carefully numbered pieces of the bark were hence removed from this tree, and as carefully put together in San Francisco. Everyone could then see the immense girth of the tree—in this case for only 21 feet of its original height. It became a celebrity overnight,

The story of Sequoia

for the incredulous public still scarcely believed the tall tales that had trickled down from the Sierras only a year or two before. Most of them were put down as the effusions of drunken gold-diggers.

San Francisco was already a seething nest of vice, and the notorious Sydney Ducks and, later, the Barbary Coast were to make the town infamous for years. Into this den of iniquity and greed, came the bark from the Sierras and the first public exhibition in the world of *Sequoia gigantea*. Fortunately we possess a record of this by a distinguished foreigner, who had already seen the trees at Calaveras.

He was William Lobb, an astute botanical collector for Messrs. Veitch of the Exotic Nursery at Chelsea, England. He sent seeds, herbarium specimens, and a living seedling toward the end of 1853, and their arrival was promptly noted in the *Illustrated London News* of February 11, 1854. They also give in full Lobb's letter to Veitch (Now Veitch and Son). Most of it is a technical description of the tree, but as to San Francisco he wrote:

> Of this vegetable monster 21 feet of the bark from the lower part of the trunk have been put in the natural form in San Francisco for exhibition; it there forms a spacious carpeted room, and contains a piano with seats for 40 persons. On one occasion 140 children were admitted without inconvenience.

Lobb's seeds of the big-tree resulted in spreading it all over England. Today, from Devon to southern Scotland there are big-trees on many estates—all about the same height and girth. Most of them average about 100 feet high, with a trunk diameter of about 4 feet. Lucky England. There are next to none on our eastern seaboard for the tree will not stand our climate. In England copious fog, coolness, rainfall,

Ever since their discovery grateful thousands have stood in awe and wonder in the groves of the big-tree. Mariposa Grove, Yosemite National Park. (Courtesy of the National Park Service)

and freedom from intense heat have resulted in this comparatively rapid growth in just over a century.

But the "sacrilegious vandals" were by no means satisfied with what had been done at San Francisco and thirsted for more marvels. In the Calaveras Grove there were many other trees, one of them larger than the despoiled one. The finest of the survivors bore the name "Mother of the Forest," a translation of an Indian name for it. It was 321 feet high, and, not counting the bark, 84 feet in circumference. Upon this luckless monster was perpetrated an infamous crime, at the behest of George D. Trask.

To save the expense of cutting it down he conceived the diabolical scheme of removing all the bark, plate by plate, for a height of 116 feet from the ground. Large augur holes were bored into the tree, and ladderlike rungs driven into them. Arrayed spirally up the trunk these rungs made it comparatively easy, if a little precarious, to get up and down, with the aid of rope slings. It was not very safe, and at least one worker fell.

Ultimately every scrap of bark was removed up to 116 feet, and carted away to Stockton for shipment via Cape Horn to New York and ultimately to London. This left the "Mother of the Forest" a stark, naked survivor doomed to an incredibly slow death. Most trees, if all the bark is taken off, even for a width of a few inches, will be dead in a year or two. Such is the vitality of the big-tree that this monument to greed lived many years.

In April, 1878, an outraged Scottish lady visited the grove, and like hundreds of others was overwhelmed at the fate of the "Mother of the Forest." She was a Miss C. F. Gordon-Cummings and likened the tree to that saint and martyr who is reputed to have survived several crops of arrows shot into him by Roman soldiers on successive days.

The story of Sequoia

Each time they took him to be dead. She wrote: "I can see her from where I sit—a ghastly object—her sides still transfixed with wooden implements of torture—the Saint Sebastian of the forest."

So ended the rape of the big-trees just after the world had first heard of them. California must still blush a little at this initial and pristine evidence of greed. Worse was to follow but so far as exhibition was concerned only two trees had been destroyed. These comprised, in 1854, the original bark specimen which had been shown in San Francisco the year before, and the much larger one taken from the "Mother of the Forest." These were shipped to New York, exhibited at two different places a few months apart, and the largest one from the "Mother of the Forest" was ultimately sent to London. Later other pieces of bark or small sections of the trunk were sent to Paris, Philadelphia, and Boston, and a huge piece went to the World's Fair in Chicago in 1893. But by that time the novelty had already worn off a bit.

Other and still more sinister interests, however, were soon attracted to the big-trees. Until finally protected, the Calaveras Grove was a shambles of destruction. Besides the trees cut or barked for exhibition there was much timber cut for lumber. Most of it was wasted because the trees in crashing down were horribly shattered and those that still had merchantable pieces could not be split into workable sections. Dynamite was used to split them, splintering a lot that was not already shattered. In fact, the wood is one of the poorest in America, brittle and easily broken, and as a result the U.S. Forest Service warned that "very much of this appalling destruction has been without leaving the owners of the Big Trees as well off as they were before it began." Unfortunately it took some years after 1854 to stop this exploitation. It took time to find out that the wood, while

These vigilant rangers in the big-tree groves protect that priceless heritage from vandalism and fire (See page 31). (Courtesy of the National Park Service)

very lasting in contact with the ground, is relatively useless as a source of lumber. Before the State of California and the U.S. National Park Service put a stop to nearly all lumbering of *Sequoia gigantea,* millions of feet were cut for vineyard stakes and shingles. A very little is still cut for furniture and tourist souvenirs.

The remarkable ability of the logs to withstand contact with the ground was convincingly demonstrated by John Muir. One *Sequoia,* when it fell, gouged a deep trenchlike depression and in this, half buried in the ground, the log had rested perhaps hundreds of years. On the top of the partly shattered log a seedling of the Silver fir had germinated and at the time Muir saw it had become a tree 380 years old. No timetable could be so accurate or prove so conclusively that the *Sequoia* log had lain there at least 380 years and, as Muir wrote, "probably thrice as long." But sections cut from the fallen trunk were "hardly distinguishable from specimens cut from living trees."

But something besides greed, gold, and timber was soon stirring in *Sequoia*-land. Just after the initial excitement had died down, and especially when the peak of the gold rush was waning, questions began to demand answers. What sort of a forest was it that produced these gigantic trees? How extensive was it? Were they found anywhere else? Why were there so few young trees among these forest giants? Did it have any relatives? How old were the trees?

Foresters, naturalists, botanists, and historians have since pieced together such a saga of *Sequoia* that few trees are known as well. But the jargon of the professionals is apt to be trying, so let us climb up into the mountains and wander in that magical forest after making proper obeisance to the experts.

three

THE BIG-TREE IN THE SIERRAS

> *The winged seeds, where they*
> *lie cold and low,*
> *Each like a corpse within its grave . . .*
> SHELLEY

HIGH IN THE COOL GRANDEUR of the Sierra Nevada we find tiny Douglas squirrels darting from tree to tree—ferocious, enterprising, sharp-toothed, greedily voracious but cannily frugal about the storage of winter food. They are the most important of all California squirrels, for their food is chiefly the small, winged seeds of the evergreens.

John Muir called this tiny ball "of fiery vigor and restlessness" the master forester of the mountains. In summer he eats his fill, but in autumn the marvelously still forest floor echoes to the muffled bombardment of cones harvested high up in the canopy by this scolding, screeching little termagant. He then cuts loose the cone scales and releases the seeds of the big-tree, the sugar pine, the firs, and other evergreens. By some immemorial instinct he plants the seeds, literally by the million, deep in the forest litter. Such a seedsman weighs scarcely a pound, for he is hardly half the size of our eastern red squirrel.

Snowbound for the winter, the big-tree seed, of which it takes ninety thousand to equal the weight of the squirrel, "lies cold and low each like a corpse within its grave." But these squirrel-planted seeds carry the miraculous potentiality of gigantism. For hidden in the cold embryo, ready to meet expectant spring, is the germ that will produce a tiny seedling, frail and puny, with as yet no hint that it may some day grow into the biggest tree in the world and one of the oldest, the fabulous big-tree of California *(Sequoia gigantea)*.

Such a fledgling planted just before Homer was born would have been perhaps twelve hundred years old at the time of Christ, nearly twenty feet in diameter and about two hundred feet high. Today it is nearly four thousand years old, at least three hundred feet high, and about thirty feet thick. Only one other living thing is as old and none other as big. One *Sequoia* is definitely known to have been just over four thousand years old, but sensational accounts of big-trees six to eight thousand years old belong to Sunday Supplement Science, not to *Sequoia*. There are today hundreds of trees ranging from twenty-five hundred to thirty-five hundred years old, and thousands of youngsters of fifteen hundred years, most of them fifteen to twenty feet in diameter.

Tree figures of height, girth, weight, and board feet are apt to be vague to those not trained to gauge them. *Sequoia gigantea* is so colossal that one feels the need to put it some-

The story of Sequoia

where, to fit it into some frame of reference. Perhaps West Tenth Street, near Fifth Avenue in New York will do as well as any.

That street is exactly 30½ feet wide, measuring from curb to curb. If it were possible to lay the trunk of the largest known *Sequoia* in that street it would not fit between the curbs. It would certainly cut off all light from the first storey windows, most of it from the second, and a good deal from the third. Turned on end it would tower above the roadway of the Golden Gate Bridge at San Francisco by a hundred feet. Its weight, when freshly cut, is over ten times that of the largest electric locomotive on the Pennsylvania Railroad.

It is difficult to believe such figures, and when the world first heard them, just over a century ago, the grandeur of the trees was matched by an avalanche of disbelief. How could nature have produced any living thing so big and old? Scientists soon quieted skepticism and today millions have visited the different groves—some in mere wonder, others to see in them a manifestation of Nature in her grandest mood, and still others to worship. Nowhere else on earth can one match the everlasting, immemorial growth of a tree against our ephemeral and haphazard passage through life. To Le Corbeau "this continuing process gives us our only approach to the conception of eternity." John Muir called them "Nature's forest masterpiece."

For us, less gifted than Le Corbeau or Muir, the mysterious cathedral-like gloom under these giant trees, the dramatic bits of sunshine filtering like some masterpiece of Chartres down onto the quiet forest floor, the stillness and the witchery, broken here and there by some venturesome squirrel, or a timid deer—could it be that *Sequoia* is California's greatest gift to the nation? High up in the Sierras they stand as Le Corbeau so well put it, as "the mirror of changeless time," the greatest evergreen tree the world has ever known.

They have however a curious distribution, both within each grove and in the state of California. Of the seventy-two known groves practically no two are contiguous, so that the groves are spotty and isolated. Quite small groves are found in the north, but the groves increase in number and density toward the south, culminating in the staggering impact of those found in Sequoia and Kings Canyon National Parks.

And unlike many evergreens the big-tree almost never occurs in pure stands. Even in some uncut and virgin groves the trees are separated by dense growths of other evergreens. In any area except the Sierra Nevada, these evergreen associates of the big-tree would be classed as magnificent trees. And they are among the finest of known evergreens. Common among them is the sugar pine, which bears the largest pine cone in the world—often twelve to eighteen inches long. Scattered, too, are stately firs and the aromatic Incense Cedar. Also common are yellow pine, white and red fir, and the white-barked pine.

But none of these ever attain the height or girth of the big-tree, which towers nearly a hundred feet or more above the canopy of its evergreen associates. John Muir, who knew these forests in their early glory, was also struck by this two-tiered canopy—the big-trees above and the evergreens below, "like slender grasses among stalks of Indian corn."

So precious and ancient a forest caused many to wonder whether the big-tree was the last and dwindling survivor of a mighty race perhaps doomed to extinction. Asa Gray, who unraveled its extraordinary antiquity, thought it was, and many less talented observers noted the paucity of new young trees. Most of these observations were made

The story of Sequoia

at the Calaveras and Mariposa groves, both of which were nearly virgin when they saw them, and reproduction of young trees was almost nil.

This failure to provide for perpetuation posed a lot of questions that have since been largely answered. Their enormous geological antiquity was ultimately well attested, but if they reproduced so poorly, how could they, through millions of years, have provided for perpetuation? Trees that fail to do so have long since passed away, such as the vegetation that produced coal and petroleum, as well as some of the fabulous ancestors of our magnolias. But *Sequoia*, which is just as ancient, has persisted in spite of the early prophets of doom. Unknown to them, their observations were largely wrong because they first saw practically virgin groves where reproduction of seedlings was next to impossible. Granted that millions of seeds were planted annually by indefatigable squirrels, why did so few ever germinate?

It is not often that conservationists and tree lovers will ultimately have to condone the ruthless and destructive tactics of the timber barons. Those in *Sequoia*-land have had about as much abuse pitched their way as any, for they were greedy and their motives never included the perpetuation of the big-tree. That their procedure has done exactly this is little credit to them but of enormous value to everyone.

Sequoia gigantea, like many other evergreens, will not, ordinarily, sprout seedlings under its own shade, nor in the acid duff of the forest floor. In nature, and without the intervention of man, its ability to reproduce and spread depends mostly upon two factors—fire and disturbance.

Fire, which practically does no harm to mature trees because of enormously thick, heat-resistant bark, has always been with *Sequoia* as in all other forests. Figures from the U.S. Forest Service show that an appreciable number of all forest fires are started by lightning.

Such fires, especially along the edges of a big-tree grove, have happened many times, some of them man-made since 1853. But for thousands of years before, a certain proportion of fires always followed lightning. From whatever cause, such fires mostly burned up the humus or duff of the forest floor, usually down to the mineral soil. It is in such exposed soils that seeds of the big-tree find a congenial place to sprout.

Their other and much more fortuitous chance came with the crashing down of an overmature tree of their own kind, or even of a rival fir or pine when they were in a *Sequoia* grove. Such a natural catastrophe digs deep furrows in the ground, up-ends a huge mass of roots and the soil clinging to them. Also, it cuts a great gap in the canopy, which lets a lot more light down onto the forest floor.

The exposure of so much mineral soil by this shattering disturbance is exactly what the seedlings need. Perhaps for the first time in centuries, such a wind-throw will be followed by hundreds of thrifty young seedlings, which grow remarkably fast for a few years, before crowding cuts most of them down.

It is these conditions of fire and disturbance that the timber interests left after them, over the protests of the civilized world. Logging machinery, skid roads, donkey engines, timber railroads, and hundreds of lusty lumberjacks—could one ask for a better setting for fire and disturbance? Both came with devastating force and continued until California and the U.S. Government put a stop to this ruthless exploitation of a priceless heritage.

The story of Sequoia

But it is precisely on these disturbed areas that the greatest growth of young *Sequoia gigantea* is now covering thousands of acres. This is so well known to professional foresters that they have even imitated the conditions created by the timber barons. The wonderful young growth of the big-tree on the Whitaker Forest, in northern Tulare County, under the supervision of the University of California, is an example of this "controlled" reproduction. There are others.

No one can condone the motives of the timber interests, but to deny the benefits that have followed would be as futile as to deplore the Renaissance because the Medici touched it off to an accompaniment of vice.

Under these conditions *Sequoia gigantea* is in no danger of extinction. The young seedlings, and even trees up to forty years of age, are peculiarly sensitive to fire. The vigilant guardians of the big-trees soon put a stop to all incipient fires, and in spite of occasional accidents, the groves are as well protected as any forest on earth.

So successful has been this intelligent campaign that the foresters are already completing studies of the proper spacing of these future forest giants. At the moment the young trees are so thick that only severe natural competition would thin them out to the required spacing. But man is interfering in this, to speed up the process of helping to capture land that rightly belongs to *Sequoia*. California has many black marks upon its record of exploitation, but the devoted rangers of the California State Parks, the U.S. Forest Service, and Sequoia and Kings Canyon National Parks are now doing a superb job in keeping out fire and promoting the perpetuation of the greatest forest trees in existence.

While this is in no sense a guidebook to *Sequoia*-land, there are features beyond the size and antiquity of the trees that cannot help raising questions. One of them is the enormous thickness of the bark. Fully mature trees will have bark from 12 to 18 inches thick. Cushionlike and heat-resistant, it has saved many a tree from fire damage and is hence one of the unique survival factors in the perpetuation of the big-trees.

The bark is ridged, dark cinnamon brown, and while very fire-resistant it is occasionally burned through as evidenced by the cavelike hollow made perhaps a century or two ago in a huge specimen called Smith's Cabin. In this hollowed-out portion of the still living tree was a "room" 16 × 21 feet. This was the home for three years of an intrepid trapper named A. J. Smith. During a furious gale, two neighboring Sequoias crashed down with earth-shaking, nerve-testing force. And as scores of huge limbs were flying through the air, Mr. Smith, crouching in his cabin, was understandably a bit nervous. Would his tree stand this disastrous hurricane? It did and the exploit is simply another illustration of the amazing vitality of a badly injured tree that survived Sierra storms for centuries.

Another but man-made injury is the tunnel cut through the famous "tunnel tree" in the Mariposa grove. Long before Mariposa was preserved from further vandalism, its owners cut a tunnel clear through a forest giant. This was wide enough to "permit a stage-load of tourists" driving through the tree. And now, after a century of such treatment, the tree is still alive and thousands of motorists drive through it every year. The tree, which may be four thousand years old, still spreads its luxuriant foliage in the lofty canopy as if in defiance of such nonsense.

Though visitors are aware of the majesty of these monolithic monsters of the forest and feel the awe that the trees inspire, they often wonder why mature specimens have no

The story of Sequoia

branches anywhere near the ground. Usually the first branch may be anywhere from a hundred and thirty to a hundred and eighty feet above the ground. As anyone can see, young big-trees thirty to forty years old will be densely clothed with foliage and branches practically down to the base. Why, later, are these all lost?

The answer is actually simple. In any evergreen forest and even in many others, the density of the canopy becomes a limiting factor in the perfectly natural pruning set up by the lack of light. In the case of the big-tree, surrounded as it is by some of its associated evergreens, the struggle for survival becomes intense. This never-ending fight for light has been going on in the Sierras for countless centuries. The tree survives, but all its lower and deeply shaded branches are what the foresters call suppressed, i.e., they wither and die off for lack of light.

Hence, as the tree grows ever upward, it loses all its lower branches and is only permitted a few when it towers over the dense evergreen canopy of its associates. Then, as if protesting its branchless centuries, it puts out its first retained branch. Many of these have been measured and vary from 7.3 to 11 feet in diameter. In one monster the total branches, not counting the foliage, weighed over 175 tons. Very few trees in the East have even *trunk* diameters to match the branches of these colossal wonders of the California mountains. Such branches do not strike one as a freak, like some gigantic wrestler. They seem perfectly in keeping in this fantastic forest, in spite of their huge size.

But transcending all statistics of height, girth, and weight, and even more absorbing than the amazing age of the individual trees was a question that remained unanswered for years. No miner at Murphy's Camp, no exploiter of bark specimens, not one of the timber scoundrels had

A giant Sequoia *in the South Calaveras Grove, Tuolumne County. This grove was added to the big-tree preserves through the generosity of John D. Rockefeller, Jr. (Courtesy of Save-the-Redwoods League)*

ever asked it. Others, however, were soon wondering where *Sequoia* came from and why was it isolated in California and nowhere else in the world. The scientists, especially, began flinging out terms like endemism, paleobotany, and a dozen other imponderables. People began asking what had all this to do with the extraordinary occurrence of *Sequoia?*

The answer did not come until the summer of 1872. Then, from a little frontier town on the Iowa side of the Mississippi River, the greatest botanist that America ever produced quietly solved the mystery. He was Dr. Asa Gray, Professor at Harvard and only recently elected president of the American Association for the Advancement of Science.

four

BEFORE THE
DAWN OF HISTORY

*"Trees and rocks will teach what thou
canst not hear from a Master."*
BERNARD OF CLAIRVAUX
(1091-1153)

DUBUQUE WAS a little uneasy in the spring of 1872, for the city fathers had just come back with the bleak tale that Clark Dodge & Company of Wall Street utterly refused to settle the town's debt of nearly nine hundred thousand dollars for a penny less than twenty-seven cents on the dollar. Some were for outright repudiation of the bonds, especially as a new threat menaced the income of this harassed little Iowa town.

It had then just about twenty thousand inhabitants

and over 175 saloons, against which its largely evangelical churchgoers launched a big temperance crusade. It failed, for as one of the aldermen dryly remarked, "if liquor was abolished Dubuque's finances would receive a deadly blow."

But things were not quite hopeless; the railway bridge had finally been built and in the summer of 1872, in spite of the staggering debt, a new red brick pavement was laid on Main Street, where at Third Street stood Paddy Sutton's saloon, one of the best in the city. Its popular proprietor divided his time between tending bar, being town policeman, and owning the cock-pit.

Smoky Illinois Central trains were already chugging through its streets, and many stern-wheelers loaded with freight were churning up the mud of the sluggish Mississippi. Two burned hotels somewhat scarred the beauty of Main Street, but the Lorimer House still stood, corn and hogs were plentiful, the lumber mill worked overtime, and the lead mines, while troubled with water, were profitable.

From those mines clay-splashed workers would gather on the sawdust-covered floor of Paddy Sutton's saloon, place their bets on the current cock-fight or prize fight and hear for the first time a whisper of what was impending for Dubuque. Certainly the pastor of the Congregational Church and other leading citizens were soon to know definitely that a distinction, having nothing to do with corn, hogs, lead, or liquor, was about to be conferred on their town.

It was hatched in Indianapolis a year before, where America's top-flight savants were holding their annual meeting in the State House. The American Association for the Advancement of Science, not then but thereafter abbreviated to AAAS, were trying to decide where the meeting for 1872 should be held. Most of them favored the

The story of Sequoia

invitation from San Francisco, the railroad to which had just been completed. But the California Academy of Sciences "could not guarantee hotels at satisfactory rates;—hence Dubuque."

This Iowa city had never before entertained such a distinguished group, and if educated Dubuque was in a dither, who could blame them? The retiring president of AAAS and principal speaker was to be Dr. Asa Gray of Harvard, certainly one of the most outstanding scholars of the nineteenth century. He had not yet quite emerged from the uproar over his advocacy of Darwin and the *Origin of Species*, a book that had split educational and religious America. It was, of course, anathema to fundamentalists in Dubuque.

It was soon known that Gray was a botanist. In those days, and even sometimes today, a botanist was caricatured as an amiable visionary with an umbrella and tin case for collecting specimens, or else he peered down the eyepiece of a microscope like a gem expert. What would the great man talk about? Some hoped it would be the local flora, for the beautiful bluffs of the Mississippi had sheets of wild flowers: violets, May-flowers, bluebells, Dutchman's breeches, shooting-star, lady's-slippers, and dozens of others.

In the meantime, responsible citizens were preparing for the meeting and they collected $2,297 to defray the expenses. This does not seem excessive, as the liquor business that year totaled half a million dollars. The Congregational and Universalist churches were set aside for the meeting, and the Lorimer Hotel for the entertainment of the scientists.

Finally in mid-August, 1872, the meeting opened. The day before Asa Gray and his wife, who was one of the most select of the proper Bostonians, saw an essentially pioneer town. Both were far too urbane and polite to contrast the amenities of Dubuque with Cambridge, and when the meeting closed, Dr. Gray spoke as follows:

> If much has been lost in not going to San Francisco, more has been gained in coming to Dubuque, for nothing could excel the overflowing kindness of the people of this small but enterprising city of the great state of Iowa.

No wonder the boosters grabbed up such felicitous notice of Dubuque. The *Daily Herald* also reported that what Gray had come to say was to be: "*Sequoia* and Its History." They were sure to have heard of the discovery of the big-tree (*Sequoia gigantea*) of the California Sierras for it had been known since 1853, but probably knew nothing of its relative, the redwood (*Sequoia sempervirens*) from the northern coast of the same state. Not one stick of redwood lumber had reached Iowa in 1872, nor was likely to until transcontinental railways became common.

What, then, could "*Sequoia* and Its History" be? Why had 164 scientists come to hear the eminent Dr. Gray? If Dubuque did not know in 1872, how many of us are better informed today? What Gray said at Dubuque had been discussed for years with his colleagues in Harvard, at the Kew Gardens in London, with John Torrey of New York, the Jardin des Plantes at Paris, and with the botanists at Geneva and Vienna.

It was, in other words, a speech that has become a classic. There was no use for "any remarks, which would now be trite, upon the size or longevity of these far-famed *Sequoia* trees." Open-mouthed crowds had already gaped at them at the Crystal Palace in London, in New York, Paris, and even in staid Boston. Gray, for the first time

The story of Sequoia

in his life, had been to California earlier that year to see them, although "until this summer I had not seen the Mississippi, nor set foot upon a prairie."

Of the majesty and awe-inspiring impact of those gigantic trees there is no hint in his speech, for his mind was on even bigger things. For in *Sequoia* he found the most spectacular refutation of the doctrine of special creation, which even Darwin had not quite killed. If, as he knew, these huge denizens of California forests had not been individually created by a possibly omnipotent being, whence came they? His explanation of their origin did not necessarily eliminate God and he quotes with evident approval a Frances P. Cobbe who in her *Darwinism and Morals* says:

> It is a singular fact, that when we can find out how anything is done, our first conclusion seems to be that God did not do it. No matter how wonderful, how beautiful, or how intimately complex and delicate has been the machinery, which has worked perhaps for centuries, perhaps for *millions of ages,* to bring about some beneficent result, if we can but catch a glimpse of the wheels, its divine character disappears.

Asa Gray did not italicize *millions of ages,* but these were the basis of his speech and it is these that make the history of *Sequoia* incomparably more significant than any tree. It was, for instance, an electrifying discovery to find a fossil *Sequoia* in England. What did that bleak little island have to do with sunny California? Questions multiplied fast when fossil ancestors of the giant big-tree and the coast redwood turned up in Alaska, Greenland (which might then have been really green), much of Europe, in North Carolina, eastern Asia, and Japan, and finally in

California itself. All this before 1872. Today we know that *Sequoia* once grew over much of the northern hemisphere. But when? And why these two relicts, now confined only to California?

Many other fossil plants and animals are completely extinct. Occasionally a few survive, as do the crocodile and the ginkgo, but who expects to see the trees that once made coal, or catch a glimpse of a dinosaur or of a living batlike "bird" with a wing-spread of twenty feet? And today one can walk comfortably through the forest-clad Sierras without once seeing a mastodon.

There was no lack of skeptics. Bits of stone upon which nature has etched an imperishable record of leaf, twig, cone, or seed—was this enough to scuttle Divine writ? Who dared, in 1872, to undermine the biblical timetable of creation with a handful of fossils? It seemed almost as sacrilegious as Bob Ingersoll, who, for God, suggested his "pail of protoplasm."

Into this atmosphere of confusion and doubt stepped the trained intellect of Asa Gray, not to undermine Christian faith, for he was himself a believer. "Let us hope . . . that in the future even more than in the past, faith in an *order*, which is the basis of science, will not (as it cannot reasonably) be severed from faith in an *Ordainer*, which is the basis of religion."

SEQUOIA AND ITS HISTORY

To walk through the isolated groves of the big-tree or the cathedral-like avenues of the coast redwood makes one wonder if Le Corbeau may not have been right. Thirty years ago this sensitive Frenchman saw in them "the mirror of changeless time." With no hint of the romanti-

The story of Sequoia

cism of Le Corbeau's *The Forest Giant,* Asa Gray attacked the incredible time element implicit in the survival of *Sequoia*. Not the age of the living trees, which was well known to be only four thousand years or so, but what had happened to those forests of *Sequoia* that throve for millions of years before this puzzling relict became isolated in California.

Any well-trained forester can detect why the redwood (*Sequoia sempervirens*) is presently confined to the fog belt of the coast, originally from Monterey nearly to Grant's Pass, Oregon. They find here moisture and coolness not to be found in the interior valleys of sun-dried California, which they shun. And for a similar reason the big-tree (*Sequoia gigantea*) is equally confined to isolated groves in the Sierras, mostly between 4000 and 7500 feet elevation. Again they demand freedom from heat and dryness and hence never invade the summer inferno of the San Joaquin Valley. Nowhere do the two trees grow together.

If they have always required coolness and moisture, where, millions of years ago, were they to find them? And who was bold enough to dogmatize as to whether their requirements then were the same as now? Puzzling questions. But Gray set out to answer them, which was possible only by intensive study of the fossil record. This he and his paleobotanical friends had done long before the Dubuque talk. They found that plant fossils were of two kinds: some revealed mere surface features such as leaf-shape and veining, stem-marking, flowers, seeds, cones, and such. But by far more important were petrifications of interior structure and even of whole trunks. For here, embalmed in imperishable stone, were the secrets of how those trees lived, their moisture requirements, and their love life. Perhaps the most dramatic of these fossilized trunks is that at the Petrified Forest of redwoods, about fifteen miles northeast of Santa Rosa, Sonoma County.

This, as Le Corbeau said, was "the sap in its evolution that took the common way of all life's forces." Dr. Gray, less poetic, found that these predawn sequoias so precisely matched the interior structure of California's present-day big-tree or redwood that there was little question of their common origin. This solved one of his problems, for it would be a hardy skeptic who could refute the evidence that form and function which so perfectly dictate the home economy of present-day *Sequoia* did not operate with like validity in the days of the dinosaurs.

To the thoughtful at Dubuque, and to us, this had somewhat intriguing implications. If, for all those millions of years, *Sequoia* was the undisputed inhabitant of the northern hemisphere, and there seems no doubt of it, how could enterprising English explorers, greedy Californian gold diggers, or pious padres have "discovered" it? Was it not better to say that we scarcely discovered *Sequoia*, but that rather late in its life it discovered us!

Gray was not diverted by such speculations, for he realized that proving the similarity of the present and ancient sequoias told us nothing of how they got to California, nor what happened to the great forests of which the present trees are mere relics.

He did not tack a timetable to the Tertiary nor construct a chronology for the Cretaceous, but he used both terms at Dubuque and so must we in understanding his "Sequoia and Its History." Briefly the Tertiary is next to the last great geological period in the history of the earth, and just precedes the Quarternary in which we now live, during which occurred the last of the great continental glaciers that covered so large a part of Europe, Asia, and

The story of Sequoia

North America. The Cretaceous is far older than the Tertiary. Recent estimates, unknown to Gray, have put the Tertiary anywhere from seventy-five to one hundred fifty million years ago and some think much more.

Sequoia has been found in strata of the Cretaceous, Tertiary, and Quarternary. In all of them, with exceptions to be noted presently, its structure is so close to the California trees that all the experts admit a common ancestry and continuous occupancy of a good part of the north temperate zone until rather recently in the Quarternary, where it became isolated in California.

The fossil record shows that from the very earliest times *Sequoia* never inherited the sex life of a still older relative, the ginkgo. This tree retained and still retains a method of reproduction wherein a motile male sex cell, only in the presence of moisture, "swims" to the expectant female cell and completes reproduction in a method strikingly like human spermatozoa. *Sequoia* never does this, although flowers, as we ordinarily understand that term, were still millions of years in the future. But flowers of a sort are represented by naked ovules found between the cone-scales of ancient and modern sequoias, in both cases fertilized by the common yellow, dustlike pollen familiar to everyone.

The problem of the immense range of the ancient and the confined isolation of modern *Sequoia* was the crux of the question. In that torrid Congregational Church at Dubuque the scientists were to hear and the world has long since pondered an explanation that modern research has scarcely modified. Heat in mid-August in Iowa is of the sort that prompts the faithful to say they can hear the corn grow. Unperturbed, the Harvard scientist lucidly unwound the evidence, which was undeniably technical. But like most great scientists he avoided the jargon of the experts, well

Many superb evergreens are intimately associated with the bigtree, among them the sugar pine, incense cedar, and some towering firs. Trinity Corners in the Giant Forest, Sequoia National Park (See page 28). (Courtesy of the National Park Service)

knowing that fancy verbiage is sometimes a cloak for ignorance.

Fossils of the redwood and the big-tree consistently show the differences found in them today. The enormous girth of the big-tree and towering height of the redwood could hardly be shown by any fossil. But their foliage and cones are significantly different, and it is these that are faithfully etched in stone. The redwood has small cones, scarcely more than an inch long, and the leaves (needles) are not pressed against the twigs, but spread to make a feathery growth. But the big-tree has cones two to three inches long and its scalelike leaves (needles) mostly hug the twigs, not unlike a juniper. These gross differences are accompanied by several technical features that need not detain us, although they are diagnostic when it comes to identifying a fossil *Sequoia,* or even a modern one.

It soon became evident that these fossil accumulations of the past could be sorted into three categories:

a those that were identical with living redwood, or so close to it that they were obviously ancestors
b those that were similarly to be identified only with the big-tree
c those which matched neither but were still, and without question, members of the genus *Sequoia,* or of the related *Metasequoia.*

Of group *c* a few had already been found when Gray talked at Dubuque, and several other fossil sequoias have been discovered since. None of these close relatives of our existing trees is now found living, except the extraordinary *Metasequoia* found as a hitherto undetected living tree in China. This had heretofore been known only as a fossil. It is, in its way, just as unique as our living *Sequoia,* but

The story of Sequoia

nothing like so impressive. It was once just as widely distributed as ancient *Sequoia,* and is now widely cultivated as an extremely interesting ornamental. Seeds were collected in the province of Hupeh, China, in 1946, and the cultivated plants are offered under the misleading names of "dawn redwood" or "living fossil."

These discoveries proved to Gray that the sequoias of California had won out in that titanic struggle for survival that is inherent in the forest ecology of all trees, a struggle lasting for millions of years, with an incalculable mortality. As Gray pieced the evidence together, there emerged bit by bit a picture of California *Sequoia,* not only as the largest and perhaps next to the oldest of living things but as the very "mirror of changeless time."

It may never be possible to say why these relatives of ancient *Sequoia* were finally extinguished, or why the fearsome animals that roamed these antediluvian forests were ultimately blotted out. But we do know that changes in topography, in the distribution of land and sea, and in the upthrust of mountain chains happened during those eons of upheaval, all of them having profound influence upon the climates of the Cretaceous, Tertiary, and Quarternary. The most recent glacial age, a mere forty or fifty thousand years ago, saw the last of many continental glaciers that crept down over nearly half of the north temperate zone.

Such a gigantic ice sheet would scrape clean all existing vegetation in its path. But in its relentless journey from the pole it would for thousands of years create at its southern margin a climatic cold front so severe that plants and animals would be driven before it, long before the actual arrival of the ice cap. This wall of ice in Manhattan, for instance, would have covered the Empire State Building, and some geologists estimate the depth of the ice sheet at

New York, over part of Long Island, and all of northern New Jersey as over two thousand feet. Such a creeping paralysis of cold covered the upper third of the United States not once but many times, making a Greenland of Manhattan, an Alaska of Chicago, and of sunny California an icy Spitzbergen. It covered Dubuque and helped to etch out the upper Mississippi.

Before such a frigid onslaught *Sequoia,* of which there were then other forms besides our two survivors, would inevitably be pushed to the southward. There, for an eon or two, they could persist in a region impossible for them today, for Kansas and Arizona and dozens of other hot dry places were then cool and moist during the all-important growing season.

The incredible pertinacity of *Sequoia* is nowhere better illustrated than in its successive migrations southward before the inexorable ice sheets, and its equally persistent retreat northward as glaciation crept poleward. Fossil *Sequoia* has been found in Alaska, Spitzbergen, Greenland, and Siberia, thousands of miles from its present home. The only things it could not endure, and does not today, are summer heat and lack of moisture.

Both trees have enormously thick bark and practical immunity to the insect pests and diseases that play havoc with so many cultivated evergreens. These may be some of the factors that contributed to survival, but many others had to be met and conquered. The big-tree, for instance, will hardly ever sprout seeds directly under a canopy of dense shade. But it and its present evergreen associates make the forest floor of cathedral-like darkness, marvelous in its cloistered stillness, but inimical to seedling big-trees. This is not true of the redwood, as we shall see in the chapter devoted to that tree.

The story of Sequoia

But they overcame this and many other vicissitudes in the long saga of this ancient titan, the modern perpetuation of which bothered Dr. Gray at Dubuque. Today, *Sequoia* has only to conquer man, for we are its last remaining enemy. That battle still goes on but its odds are now in favor of *Sequoia* as a result of its protection from fire and slaughter.

Dr. Gray knew well that some of the southern migrations of *Sequoia* and its recessions toward the pole came long before the cataclysmic upheavals that thrust up the giant Sierras or the coast mountain ranges. But at the last and what we fondly suppose is the final recession of the ice, the California mountains were already in existence.

It was at the end of this last ice age that the stage was set for what we find today. Gradually, as conditions became more possible, the various ancestors of the present sequoias became isolated by factors of climate that persist today. The coast redwood is now and was then confined to something like its present limits in the fog belt of northern California. The big-tree, which will stand winter cold and much snow, but not summer heat, was gradually isolated at those elevations in the Sierras that provide such conditions. So selective is it that it grows at lower elevations in the northern part of its range, but at higher ones in its southern limits. Nowhere did it survive in the heat and drought of the San Joaquin Valley.

No one knew better than Dr. Gray that the above explanation is a vast oversimplification of what actually happened. For both species of *Sequoia* have now and had then active competition for all the light, food, soil moisture, and other things that forest trees demand besides their basic climatic necessities. Of these competitors the incense cedar, various pines, and some firs vastly outnumber the big-tree in the Sierras, so much so that isolated groves of the big-tree are all that are left, surrounded by far denser growths of actively spreading evergreens. Many of these are tolerant of shade, will germinate at least some of their seeds in forest humus, and in all ways seem better suited for survival than *Sequoia gigantea*.

What rear-guard actions there must have been for the final capture of this prevailingly evergreen high Sierra, no one can tell today. Both *Sequoia gigantea* and its evergreen associates are confined to such climatically isolated regions. But *Sequoia* not only won its last battle, but had been fighting similar battles for millions of years before. In California all other closely related species of *Sequoia*, except the coast redwood, were eliminated in that climactic struggle. The survivors stand today as the epitome of eons of effort, the last relics of vanished days, solitary sentinels of the past.

Equally dynamic were the factors that finally isolated the coast redwood *(Sequoia sempervirens)* to its present home, at about the same time. In this case the isolation is much more extensive, for the historical limits of the tree stretch from near Monterey for about five hundred miles to southern Oregon. It is practically confined to the fog belt, will not stand winter cold, scarcely ever sees snow, and is much more luxuriant in its reproduction than the big-tree. And the redwood, before cutting decimated it, was found in almost pure stands, vastly outnumbering the big-tree which, now that exploration has uncovered all of them, comprises only seventy-two isolated groves, nowhere continuous.

The existing trees are probably older and certainly larger than any living thing. But their size and age pale beside their history, and as Asa Gray unfolded that story at Dubuque he had this to say:

The story of Sequoia

Order and exquisite adaptation did not wait for man's coming, nor were they ever stereotyped. Organic nature—by which I mean the system and totality of living things, and their adaptation to each other and to the world—with all its apparent and indeed real stability, should be likened, not to the ocean, which varies only by tidal oscillations from a fixed level . . . , but rather to a river, so vast that we can neither discern its shores nor reach its sources, whose onward flow is not less actual because it is too slow to be observed by the *ephemerae* which hover over its surface, or are borne upon its bosom.

Asa Gray was sixty-two when he talked at Dubuque; now he is safely enshrined in the Hall of Fame. But by 1872 he had already made Cambridge a Mecca for botanists from all over the world. Unlike most of them, he combined a staggering dose of technical knowledge with a highly speculative and philosophical turn of mind.

"Sequoia and Its History" not only took the trees from the frank charlatanism of the Crystal Palace in New York and London, both of which had exploited this California wonder, but with it Gray opened up vistas of the mind. He knew well that to overwhelmingly fundamentalist America "Such ideas as these, though still repugnant to some, and not long since to many . . . ," would ultimately prevail. Today they are a truism, but at Dubuque Gray took *Sequoia* from those who knew it only as another California marvel, perhaps like gold or San Francisco harbor. He made these trees a symbol of an ageless miracle, reaching back to the origin of most flowering plants, millions of years before man was invented. Then came the timeless struggle for survival and the final isolation in California. More, perhaps, than he realized, Gray at Dubuque emphasized the dictum of Bernard of Clairvaux, who wrote in the eleventh century that "Trees and rocks will teach what thou canst not hear from a Master."

Dubuque heard a master that day, but there is no record that it made much of a flutter. The town did realize, however, that even the loftiest savants need a little diversion, and an evening or two later staged a party for them and their wives.

It was the "most brilliant gathering Dubuque has ever witnessed and probably its like will not be seen again. . . . There was a choice company of Dubuque's best citizens and a fine representation of the best scientific brains of the country." The alert reporter of the *Daily Herald* noted ice cream and cake as refreshments; that "young sprigs of man and maidenhood" . . . were soon dancing the waltz, but for the most part "decorous professors eluded the witcheries of Terpsichore."

Among them was Asa Gray with the manuscript of "Sequoia and Its History" in his pocket, soon to leave for Cambridge and the nearest thing to immortality that a scientist is likely to achieve.

While Gray had talked mostly about the giant trees in the Sierras he also, of course, had to mention the other *Sequoia,* similarly confined to California. And no one would be quicker than that state to remind us that the big-tree is by no means all the *Sequoia* story. Down along the coast, and in far greater numbers, grows another kind, famous throughout the world as the source of redwood and known to science as *Sequoia sempervirens.* Ever since their discovery millions have stood in speechless awe before these twin evidences of California's priceless heritage to the nation.

five

THE REDWOOD

THE TALLEST EVERGREEN tree in the world is one of the most elusive. Stretching for nearly 500 miles along the coast of California and southern Oregon, and ten times more numerous than the big-trees, it completely avoided detection for over two hundred years after California was first discovered.

Many Spanish and Portuguese navigators were along that magical coast, even as early as 1539. Juan Rodriguez Cabrillo, who first saw the California coast on September 28, 1542, can be exonerated for not seeing the tree for he first landed too far south. There is a vague suggestion that Cabrillo went as far north as Fort Ross, and of his naming the heavily wooded region around it "El Cabo de Pinos." These "pines" were in all probability redwoods, but Cabrillo appears to have been a better navigator than botanist so that his "discovery" of redwood is highly questionable.

The spraylike needles and cones of the redwood, Sequoia sempervirens. (*Natural size*)

But how could Sir Francis Drake, in 1579, have missed it? He spent several weeks in what is now Drake's Bay, and went into the interior, while one of his beached ships was overhauled. He noted several strange animals, but either did not see or failed to notice a tree twice as high as any in England. He named the country New Albion and his bay is only about twenty miles from the world-famous Muir Woods. Furthermore, in what is now Marin County, into which Drake penetrated, there were then plenty of redwoods, but Drake did not take any notice. Years later the Russians were not so obtuse.

It would seem almost impossible that the Viscaino expedition, which landed at Monterey in 1602-3, could have failed to see the redwoods. This splendidly equipped party was provided with two devout padres, who hastily built an altar and said mass under "a tall oak." Redwoods were all around them but they make no mention of them.

All of this was long before San Francisco and its incomparable harbor was discovered by Don Manuel Ayala in 1775. It then, of course, belonged to Spain. Finally breaking the exploratory blindness of all his predecessors was Fray Juan Crespi, the very talented scribe of the Portola expedition, which had been sent from New Spain (Mexico) to establish missions in what was then called Upper California.

Crespi was the first white man to see the redwoods and note the fact. He wrote, under the date of October 16, 1769, that they found the tree on the Pajaro River, near the modern town of Watsonville, which is on the bay of Monterey. They knew of the bay from the Viscaino expedition of 1602-3. Crespi not only saw the tree but described it. He said that the plains and hills were:

The story of Sequoia

Well forested with very high trees of a red cedar, not known to us. They have a very different leaf from cedars, and although the wood resembles cedar somewhat in color, it is very different and has not the same odor; moreover the wood of the trees that we have found is very brittle. In this region there is great abundance of these trees and because none of the expedition recognizes them they are named redwood from their color.

Actually what Crespi saw was a relatively small stand of this fabulous evergreen, which does not become common until one reaches the San Francisco Bay area, of which few now remain. And its greatest magnificence and density are reached only in the northern part of the state. With Crespi on the Portola expedition was Miguel Costanso who wrote in his diary, in October, 1769, that the redwoods were "the largest, highest and straightest trees that we had seen up to that time; some of them were four or five yards in diameter. The wood is of a dull dark reddish color, very soft, brittle and full of knots." Perhaps Costanso should share with Crespi the honor of being the discoverer of the redwood.

It was many years later before California realized the stupendous implications of its redwood forests. These ultimately came to bear the same relation to its economic life that the white pine did to New England: incalculable wealth. A few of the Spaniards had cut some redwood timber and the saintly Junipero Serra, who might be called the father of San Francisco, ordered on his deathbed that his coffin was to be made of redwood. This was unearthed ninety-eight years after his burial and found to be in perfectly sound condition. Some timber was also shipped by

THE AGELESS RELICTS

the enterprising Spaniards to make boats for Society Island pearl divers, and for other uses.

But the great exploitation of redwood did not come until the Gold Rush of 1849. Considerably before this the Russians began lumbering redwood near Bodega Bay, at Fort Ross, and along the Russian River. And a Russian church built of redwood at Fort Ross in 1812 still stands. But the total cut of timber by the Russians might be compared to the difference between a three-storey house and the Empire State Building. In any case the Mexican Government, which then owned California, was much relieved when the Russians left in 1841.

In less than nine years the rape of the redwoods was already well under way. Sawmills only a short distance north of San Francisco, in Marin County, were already operating in the very region where Sir Francis Drake had failed to see the tree. In the mushrooming city, with its hordes of gold seekers, the demand for redwood timber was all but limitless. Banks, stores, churches, houses, and bridges were hastily thrown up and often as hastily burned down in several incendiary fires. These, of course, merely tripled the demand for redwood.

Its great value as lumber had been known to the Indians for centuries. From it they made canoes, their sweathouses, and simple dwellings. Its resistance to decay was well known to them, to the Russians, and ultimately to our timber barons. From the time of the Gold Rush until about 1917 the fury of exploitation was so great that conservationists have never ceased to rage.

That rage was entirely justified, but it was largely based on the cupidity and greed of the early loggers. It must not be forgotten that the United States had no control over California until we took it over from Mexico in 1848.

The story of Sequoia

Two years later the state became part of the Union, but this was many years before we had a National Forest service and before the creation of our National Parks.

From 1848 until about 1917 there was hence ruthless exploitation of perhaps the finest stand of evergreen timber on earth. Crooks were common both in and out of the government, faked homesteaders were numerous, their holdings, sometimes worth millions, were a gambler's paradise, and huge lumber companies ultimately grabbed hundreds of thousands of acres of virgin timber. There was then no one to stop them, for the U.S. Government had no jurisdiction over California land and there was no valid law to prevent an owner from selling his trees.

It is easy in 1962 to deplore what happened in the past. Professor Samuel J. Record in his *Timbers of the New World* estimated that the total redwood forest was about one million acres. Later estimates have considerably increased this. The average yield per acre varies from a high of about one million board feet to a low of perhaps half a million board feet. And even from cut-over redwood the second growth timber frequently yields enormous amounts of lumber. Professor Emanuel Fritz of the University of California, the Number One expert on redwood, has estimated that the ultimate yield on the half million acres of cut-over, selectively logged forest should be somewhere near 500 million board feet per year.

Such figures are astronomic. A tabulation based largely on the best estimates would show:

Natural area of redwood: at least one million acres, and recent estimates go as high as 1.6 million acres.
Amount already harvested: about half a million acres.

Average yield
> FROM VIRGIN TIMBER: 1 million to half a million board feet per acre.
>
> FROM CUT-OVER LAND: varies greatly depending on logging methods, freedom from fire, etc., but in fifty years it is a very large total.
>
> Final exhaustion of virgin redwood: about eighty to one hundred years hence.

All of which adds up to the staggering value of California redwood and to the fact that some of the lumber companies and a few individuals accumulated princely fortunes.

No one can condone their logging methods, nor forgive the crookedness of the earlier timber barons, but some of the more ardent and often quite naïve conservationists appear to have ignored one basic fact. Redwood, like petroleum, is one of the natural resources of the state, and without either of them the economy would be sadly jolted. In other words, redwood is a legitimate source of wealth, and all that is needed is to protect this fabulous natural gift.

That consummation is at least partly on the way. The more responsible lumber companies now have professional foresters on their staffs. They have set aside huge tracts of cut-over redwood, where proper management and freedom from fire will ultimately provide a tremendous annual yield of lumber. One such tract is over one hundred thousand acres.

In other words, California has emerged from its infancy of greed and exploitation and there is a well-defined tendency to correct their early errors. This may well result in the cut-over areas becoming a legitimate source of annual

The story of Sequoia

wealth. Otherwise they would become shattered shambles, following clear cutting, burning of slash, and final erosion.

The danger of total destruction of virgin redwood will, in any case, be long delayed, for all the experts agree that only about half the total stand has been cut. The cut of the lumber companies is roughly estimated at about 500 million board feet per year. Some perhaps overly optimistic estimates indicate that there remains of uncut timber 50 billion board feet. And even the U.S. Forest Service has estimated the uncut redwood at 31 billion board feet.

In 1917 cutting was in full swing and it appeared that the end was altogether too close. This would mean that California might some day wake up to the appalling fact that, while redwood lumber was known all over the world, the state had done nothing to preserve the trees that produced it.

Hence, in 1920 was born an intelligently managed, dedicated institution called Save-the-Redwoods League. It was founded by three men, Henry Fairfield Osborn and Madison Grant, both of New York, and John C. Merriam, a naturalist of Iowa. None of them was a forester, but scarcely any other Americans except Gifford Pinchot and Theodore Roosevelt were so fired with the idea that California had a priceless natural heritage and that something must be done about it.

Soon after, many Californians joined the League; today it has thousands of members from all over the country. From gifts, annual dues, and bequests it has raised several million dollars, which are matched by equal sums provided by the California State Parks system. It all adds up to the purchase and dedication forever of some of the finest natural redwood forests, totaling about 70 thousand acres. There is also the world-famous Redwood Highway, ap-

A trail through the redwoods in the Muir Woods National Monument, the nearest protected grove to San Francisco. (Courtesy of the National Park Service)

propriately called Avenue of the Giants Parkway where it goes through the best of these forests. A listing of the main reservations will be found in chapter eight.

The nearest redwood grove to San Francisco is the famous Muir Woods, which was set aside as a National Monument by President Theodore Roosevelt in 1908. It was a gift to the nation of Mr. and Mrs. William Kent, and now comprises 485 acres.

The League should have the unstinting support of all conservationists and of everyone else who appreciates the majesty and awe of these incomparable evergreens. Its permanent address is: Save-the-Redwoods League, 114 Sansome Street, San Francisco 4, California.

THE TREE

Most loyal Californians are apt to say that the redwood is the tallest tree in the world. Equally loyal Australians are just as sure that one of their *Eucalyptus* trees is taller still. As only a few feet are involved, Californians would be on safer ground to say that redwood is the tallest *evergreen* on earth. Many of them are 350 feet high and one has been measured as 364 feet high. Diameters of twenty feet are rare, but thousands of them have diameters from fourteen to sixteen feet.

Hence the redwood is taller than the big-tree but smaller in girth and it does not live as long. As we have seen the big-tree sometimes reaches an age of four thousand years, but the oldest redwood is usually a little less than half this; sometimes considerably less. One, however, preserved at Richardson Grove, was twenty-two hundred years old. But it has one incomparable advantage over the big-tree; in a primeval forest it may have no lateral branches for

The story of Sequoia

two hundred feet, and its huge bole tapers only slightly. In other words its yield of lumber is gigantic: a single tree may provide 490 thousand board feet of lumber. A single acre of timber yielded enough lumber to build twenty-two houses.

The redwood differs also from the big-tree in the profusion and relative speed of its reproduction. The big-tree, as we have seen, is a bit erratic in its method of perpetuation. But the sprout-trees and true seedlings of redwood are so prolific that the tree was very appropriately christened *Sequoia sempervirens,* literally ever or always green. Its dense foliage and the myriads of sprout-trees and the real seedlings make redwood forests ever and profusely green.

Its foliage differs, too, from the big-tree. The redwood has many expanded needles in a flat, spraylike cluster, not very different from our Eastern hemlock. The individual needles on mature shoots are ½ to ¾ inch long, about ⅛ inch wide, green and shiny above, but with two lighter bands beneath. The needles, which live three or four years, do not drop individually, as in most evergreens, but fall with the spraylike cluster. The forest floor is thus always littered with these already useless sprays of foliage. So stealthy and so slow is this shedding of the foliage sprays that the tree is never denuded and is truly ever green.

None of this foliage is found on mature trees except high up in the canopy, which is so dense that little light filters down to the forest floor. The incredibly tall and very straight trunks are covered with thick, spongy reddish-cinnamon-colored bark, often a foot thick and highly fire-resistant. Also up in the canopy are borne the small cones, which are roundish and a little less than one inch long. Among its scales are the tiny winged seeds.

While few seeds ever germinate among the five million that a mature tree will annually produce, enough do so to provide a constant reseeding. The seedlings are nearly immune to the darkness of the forest floor, and, if protected from fire, will provide a crop of young trees. But competition for light and ultimate suppression for the lack of it much limits the ultimate crop. It is literally a case of millions being called but only a few being chosen. If redwood depended only on true seedlings its survival might be a bit precarious as it is in many other evergreen virgin forests.

But Nature has endowed the tree with an extraordinary alternative. Unlike practically all other evergreens, it will sprout freely from a cut stump, from fire-scarred trees, and even from fallen logs. Anywhere from scores of to several hundred sprouts will burgeon and live for the first year on the nourishment from its stump or log. It will, however, make its own set of roots and become a full-fledged sprout tree. There are, at first, millions of such, but they too are killed off by competition. The surviving sprout-trees are so numerous, however, that, with the seed trees, the ultimate survival of redwood is assured.

Another source of sprout-trees is the burl of the redwood. These wart-like protuberances are found near the base of the trunk and vary from the small ones sold to tourists to huge "warts" several feet in diameter. Both large and small burls have the capacity for producing many shoots, as every tourist has found when the apparently inert burl is put in a dish of water. The big burls may produce scores or even hundreds of such feathery shoots, which also make roots of their own and add to the profusion of redwood reproduction.

Because of the vast number and the majesty of mature trees and the lavish exuberance of its dual method of re-

The story of Sequoia

production, the redwood forest is unlike any other on earth. One of its most perceptive admirers is Donald Culross Peattie. In his *Natural History of Western Trees* he writes of the dramatic contrast as one leaves the staring color of California's farmland and enters a redwood forest:

> Then suddenly you are enfolded in the first of the centenarian groves, and for the next 40 miles, to and through the Avenue of the Giants, you are seldom out of their ancient shade. The transition is like stepping into a cloister, one infinitely more spacious and lofty than any ever raised by man, and closing the door behind you upon the bright secular world. Young and old, every visitor, falls abruptly silent; cars creep slowly, the drivers conscious of the sacrilege of speed.

As the survival of the redwoods as well as of the bigtree has been noted in Chapter IV, it is needless to emphasize here the enormous geological antiquity of the redwoods. Their survival since the last Ice Age, however, is based on a peculiar set of climatic factors.

It is a commonplace to say that the redwoods are found only in the fog belt of coastal California. That is true but not completely so. Careful ecological studies in the mountains near Monterey show that even if there is a daily envelopment of fog, the redwood without adequate rainfall is poor or lacking. It is true that these hills are practically at the southern edge of the tree's range. And as one goes northward the trees become much denser, taller, and fantastically luxuriant.

As one goes north along the coast the daily fogs are denser. And rainfall in the coast range gradually increases from sixty inches to a hundred inches a year near the Oregon border. It is this combination of heavy rainfall and daily

The towering boles of the redwood in the Prairie Creek Redwoods, comprising over 9000 acres in Humboldt County. (Courtesy of Save-the-Redwoods League)

fog that has made the redwood forests of Del Norte, Humboldt, Mendocino, and Sonoma counties the finest in the world. And it is mostly in these four counties that the vigilant Save-the-Redwoods League has set aside their priceless reservations.

The redwood empire thus stretches from just south of Monterey, where its occurrence is not very impressive, northward into extreme southern Oregon, where there is perhaps somewhat less than two thousand acres of it. Stretching for about five hundred miles in length, the width of the redwood forest varies only from ten to about forty miles, usually about half the latter figure. Nowhere does it inhabit the hot, dry valleys behind the Coast Range, and in many places it fails to occur along the shore. Its finest stands are always in the river valleys and flats, and except on the highest peaks of the Coast Range it never sees snow. Nor is this redwood empire ever really hot.

It is this combination of its need for coolness and moisture that has made redwood cultivation precarious in the East and impossible in the prairie states. The few that have survived culture along the Atlantic seaboard are mere caricatures of the originals. Trees planted about the same time in England, however, are already one hundred feet high.

Most visitors who travel on the Redwood Highway or along the Coast Road are puzzled at the absence of logging. These famous roads go through some of the finest redwoods in existence, but the huge lumbering industry is mostly along secondary roads, often mere logging trails. There is no secrecy about this, but the cutting of huge trees is a hazardous job even for the experts. Casual visitors are not totally unwelcome, but the timber people urge the inexperienced to keep out of a region where a falling titan may weigh hundreds of tons.

The story of Sequoia

Perhaps because the redwood has been known ever since 1769, and its lumber is valued all over the world, the tree has never suffered the indignities heaped upon its big brother up in the Sierras. While redwood was piling up fortunes, the still more fabulous big-tree was carted off to New York and London to let the public gape at a woodland monster.

six

THE BIG-TREE IN NEW YORK AND LONDON

A TRIO OF MALE PRIMA DONNAS dominated the press and amusements of New York about a century ago. One of them founded on March 2, 1834, the original version of *The New Yorker,* and called it that, but after seven pretty lean years it quietly folded. Nothing daunted by his failure with the first *New Yorker,* Horace Greeley then became the owner and editor of the *New York Tribune,* which was rather quickly a thumping success.

The second of the trio was the rambunctious James Gordon Bennett who, in 1841, had offered Greeley the chance to share in establishing the *New York Herald.* Greeley turned it down and was ever after hounded by the *Herald,* not only as a prohibition humbug, but because the *Tribune* cribbed too much foreign news from Bennett's more enterprising *Herald.*

The story of Sequoia

The third and by far the most notorious of the trio was P. T. Barnum, who in that yeasty year of 1841, when Bennett started the *Herald* and Greeley the *Tribune,* bought Scudder's American Museum on lower Broadway. He soon transformed this into the American Museum of Curios, brought over Tom Thumb from England, and took more advertising space in both the *Herald* and the *Tribune* than all other amusements combined. In spite of this largesse the rampageous Mr. Barnum was hated by Bennett and distrusted by Greeley.

Not one of that trio suspected in 1852 that two of them were to be mixed up in the greatest fiasco that had ever happened to New York, or that Bennett's *Herald* would be the only newspaper in New York to pan the efforts first of Barnum and then of Greeley to put some sense into the New York Crystal Palace. This was constantly tottering on the verge of bankruptcy. And no one could be expected to know that a hitherto undiscovered tree from the Sierras of California would ultimately come to New York and postpone at least for one more season the imminent debacle up at Sixth Avenue and 40th Street.

This costly monster of glass and metal had been set up in what is now Bryant Park, the east end of which was then occupied by the Croton Reservoir, now the site of the Public Library. It was the fond delusion of its stockholders and a flock of anxious creditors that our Crystal Palace would duplicate the amazing success of the much larger one in London, which in 1851 housed what amounted to a World's Fair. The Bryant Park venture never did, and Bennett thought it never would if Barnum or Greeley had anything to do with it.

The Palace was scheduled to be opened in May, 1853. One peppery exhibitor from England came here in April, but the building was nowhere near ready, so he took his exhibit back and wrote in the *Times* of London, June 27, 1853, "In fact the Americans are quite ashamed of it—you never hear the subject named, and it is looked upon as a stock-jobbing affair, originated by a few speculators." This was not quite true, for the originators of the scheme were responsible New Yorkers, with a plentiful sprinkling of such names as Mortimer, Sedgwick, Livingston, Torrey, White, Greeley, etc. But most of them were rank amateurs in catching the public fancy, and they had plenty of competition, for showmanship was no stranger to New York in the 1850's. Barnum had already imported the Swedish Nightingale, who took the town by storm. No songstress before or since ever created such a furor as did Jenny Lind.

The town also sported two opera companies, three simultaneous showings of Uncle Tom's Cabin, nightly parties at Niblo's Gardens and Donetti's Acting Monkeys.

This made pretty tough going for the Crystal Palace. Maddening delays postponed its opening. What was happening to it finally provoked the *Times on* May 7, 1853, to editorialize thus:

> We warn the authorities against permitting this indiscriminate growth of taverns around the Crystal Palace. Half its attraction, half its beauty will vanish if these poisonous fungi are allowed to grow undisturbed around its base.

The *Times* had warned on March 25 that the

> . . . prospect at present does not present the most inviting appearance—vacant lots, ragged rocks, deep pits with relics of country shanties.

After terrific efforts by the management, and with many of its exhibits not yet unpacked, it was finally opened

The story of Sequoia

by President Fillmore on July 14, 1853. The only way of getting there was by what they called the Sixth Avenue Railway, which meant the horse cars, or by omnibus, and the traffic ploughed its way "through mud or dust six to eight inches deep."

There were soon ominous rumblings, however, that all was not well with the Crystal Palace in spite of its grandiose opening. Counterfeit tickets popped up, attendance after the first fanfare rapidly dwindled, and it was obliged to close in the fall. The management had also neglected to announce the jury awards to the exhibitors and Bennett's *Herald* on January 7, 1854, wanted an explanation. Its editorial: "We suspect that their concealment is another evidence of mismanagement which has characterized the whole proceedings of the Crystal Palace Company."

Creditors soon became clamorous and one of them on March 22, 1854, got an injunction from the Supreme Court, the object of which, according to the *Times*, "is to close the Crystal Palace, and wind up its business for the benefit of its creditors." Perhaps anticipating that suit, the directors on March 6 unanimously chose Barnum as President.

It was obvious to Barnum that something must be done if the Palace was to open during the season of 1854. With characteristic audacity he announced in all three newspapers for April 27 that the world-famous Henry Ward Beecher would be the orator at the reopening on May 4, and that a prize ode would be read by its author, William Ross Wallace.

With much oratory the Palace opened all right on May 4 amid a blast of publicity and reams of advertising. What Mr. Bennett thought of these proceedings is shown by the *Herald* of May 5, which stated:

For a full and particular account of this great affair,

read Falstaff's account of the march of his troops through Coventry—Vide Shakespeare.

The rest of the New York papers devoted all of page one and a lot of other space to it, as many people thought that the only hope for the Crystal Palace was Barnum. Attendance did increase by virtue of thinking up all the catch-penny devices known to showmanship.

While all this was stirring up the dust in Sixth Avenue, no one noticed the following advertisement in the *Herald* of April 29, 1854:

> The big tree, from California—ready for exhibition on the 8th of May. The immense tree recently felled upon the Sierra Nevada, California, has at length arrived in the city of New York, where it is placed for public exhibition in the spacious Racket Court, adjoining the Metropolitan Hotel, Broadway. This gigantic monarch of the forest measured, while standing, three hundred and twenty feet in height, and ninety five feet in circumference. Its age has been estimated at three thousand years. It was first exhibited at San Francisco, where the interior formed a spacious carpeted room, containing a piano, with seats for forty persons. On one occasion one hundred and forty children were admitted, without inconvenience; and, at another time, thirty-two couples waltzed within its colossal enclosure. The tree was felled by means of large pump augurs, requiring the labor of ten men for twenty-six days, at an expense of five hundred dollars, besides the immense cost of removing it on ship board, and transporting it hither. This is the same tree described in a February number of the London Illustrated News, Gleason's Pictorial, of October and March last, and noticed by several of the leading journals. It was likewise seen standing in its natural state by Senator Gwin, Mr. Adams,

The story of Sequoia

of the Express Company, and several other gentlemen, whose certificates will vouch for its identity. This is the first time it has ever been offered for exhibition since it left San Francisco. The bark was stripped from the tree for the length of fifty feet from the base, and is from one to two feet in thickness. It was taken off in sections, so that it can be placed, relatively, in its original position, and thus give the beholder a just idea of the gigantic dimensions of the tree. So placed, it occupies a space of about thirty feet in diameter, or ninety feet in circumference, and fifty feet in height. A piece of wood will be shown which has been cut from the tree across the whole diameter.

Absolutely nothing happened for a month, when the *Times* on June 1 and the *Herald* on May 30 both carried modest little ads that the tree "will be exhibited *for the first time in the Atlantic States,* this day and evening."

This didn't disturb Barnum or the Crystal Palace and the delay in this first showing of the big-tree in New York may have been prophetic of what was to happen. A certain Captain W. H. Hanford, who was the promoter of this first showing of *Sequoia gigantea,* had far too formidable a rival when it came to tickling the fancy of New Yorkers about a century ago. His original timing was poor, as his opening date of May 8 for the big-tree was too near Barnum's of May 4 for the Palace. Hanford decided to let the Crystal Palace excitement die down a bit, but it did not save his show, which failed within a short time. The bark was finally put in a warehouse and with the burning of this came the end of the first attempt to show this wonder of California to New York.

Meanwhile, the Crystal Palace was in a precarious position. Even the genius of Mr. Barnum failed to rescue

Crystal Palace, in what is now Bryant Park, New York City. The ruin of this costly fiasco was postponed one more year by the summer of 1855. (See pages 82 and 83). (Courtesy of Travel Magazine*)*

it, as its handicaps were too heavy. He resigned as President, and it was reported that it would close for good on October 31, 1854. The next day the *Times* announced that "During the removal of the goods and the sales at auction within the Palace, visitors will be admitted at 12½¢ each." This looked like the end if anything did.

The Palace did not close, however, and Horace Greeley took over the presidency for the season of 1855. It was so pinched for funds that it found itself unable to pack and ship some of the art works loaned from France, which it had agreed to do gratis if they were not sold.

Greeley, who was in Paris on behalf of his *Tribune,* was soon to learn that French artists thought American promises should mean something more than words. One particularly volatile sculptor had the great Mr. Greeley thrown into jail as a common fraud. After all, was he not the president of the Palace, which had just repudiated its obligation to return unsold art? The glee of James Gordon Bennett in the *Herald* was unbounded.

It was all patched up by the French Government agreeing to pay the freight. Greeley came home to a practically denuded Crystal Palace, for everyone admitted that French art was one of its chief distinctions.

By June 1, 1855, the place was in such a state that the *Times* said in an editorial, "The interior of the Crystal Palace is fast becoming a beggarly array of empty space." It was soon to be filled and the Palace rescued from the ever-threatening bankruptcy that had always hung over it —at least for the season of 1855.

In the amusement advertisements of all the leading daily papers of New York, on July 3, 1855, there appeared the following:

The story of Sequoia

The Tree Mastodon: A mountain of wood—a single tree taller by a hundred feet than the Bunker Hill monument. Great attraction at the Crystal Palace—The Monarch of the California Forest, supposed to be the largest tree in the world, has arrived at this port from San Francisco, and will be exhibited in the Crystal Palace, the only building in New York large enough to contain it on and after the

FOURTH OF JULY

This giant tree has been named by botanists, *Washingtonia gigantea*. It measured when standing 363 feet from base to summit. Its diameter is 31 feet at the base and 15½ feet at the distance of 116 feet from the roots. No big tree ever exhibited and none of its race remaining in California compare with this Sylvan Mastodon, or as it was called by the California Indians in their language the "Mother of the Forest." The Crystal Palace has been rented at a vast expense for the exhibition, which transcends in interest all the marvels for which California is celebrated. Doors open 8 A.M. until 8 P.M. Admission is 25 cents. N. B. Hayward's splendid Quadrille Band will be in attendance.

This "Mother of the Forest" was, of course, the one that had been stripped of its bark near Murphy's Camp, Calaveras County, California. News of the discovery of *Sequoia gigantea* had gone all over the world long before it was possible to get this sample from the heights of the Sierra Nevada.

For the New York of 1855 the results of the advertisement were prodigious. The *Tribune* on July 6 carried another advertisement which said that "This enormous sample of the 'Tall Timber' of California attracted upwards of six thousand persons on the Fourth of July." After repeating a good deal of the first advertisement, they closed with what was certainly a true statement: "This phenomenon of the vegetable kingdom is creating as much astonishment among scientific men as among the community at large." It was no wonder, for the world had not then seen a tree the trunk of which would scarcely fit into an average city street, and was already a thousand years old at the time of Christ.

So successful was the exhibit that the advertisements were repeated in all the leading New York papers throughout July. One of them in the *Times* for July 10, embellished the tale by saying that the growing tree had an altitude "equal to that of the third Pyramid of the Nile." ·

Nor was all the newspaper publicity confined to paid advertisements. The *New York Evening Express* wrote in its news columns: "The big-tree exhibited in this city, several months ago, was almost a pigmy in comparison with this mastodon." Even the more staid *Evening Post*, in its issue of July 7, 1855, said:

> The Tree Mastodon: A mountain of wood—a single tree taller by a hundred feet than the Bunker Hill Monument, and about as thick at the base, now occupies the Crystal Palace! It is from California and is called *Washingtonia gigantea*. All "big-trees" heretofore exhibited were pigmies to this tower of timber.

This was also an evident reference to the ill-starred Hanford venture of 1854.

Crowds continued to pour into the Palace, perhaps because the advertisements toward the end of July stated that the tree would be "on exhibition for a short time . . . previous to its departure for the Crystal Palace in London." This appeared in all New York papers almost daily until

The story of Sequoia

August 27. Then on August 30 the *Times* carried the announcement that "The exhibition of this unequalled Monarch of the Forest will close on the first of October next." The latter was repeated in all papers almost daily up to September 19.

It is no exaggeration to say that the Crystal Palace was saved by *Sequoia*, for it was practically the only attraction in the summer of 1855, and without it the Palace would certainly have closed. Its savior, if he really was one, was the Mr. George D. Trask, who was responsible for the original debarking of the "Mother of the Forest." Nothing daunted by that dastardly act, he appeared apprehensive that no one would believe him. It is quite true that stripping 60 tons of bark from 116 feet of a forest giant in the high Sierras seemed incredible. At any rate he induced an unimpeachable witness to verify the facts. He was Alvin Adams of Adams and Company's Express, who testified, in part, as follows:

> . . . At the time I visited the said grove Mr. Trask was engaged in taking the bark from one for the purpose of exhibiting it in the Atlantic States and Europe, and to the best of my knowledge and belief, the one now on exhibition at the Crystal Palace in the City of New York, is the same identical tree which I then saw, the bark of which I know to have been removed. Given under my hand and seal this 15th day of August, 1855. Alvin Adams.

The conservationists were still furious over Trask's debarking of the "Mother of the Forest," but nearly everyone admits that without *Sequoia* the dwindling and ill-starred venture on Sixth Avenue would have folded at the end of 1854. In the autumn of 1855 Trask packed up his bark and sailed for London. On October 5, 1858, with a final flare of futility, the Crystal Palace in New York was completely destroyed by fire.

LONDON

When Trask landed there was not a building in London large enough to house his tree. The obvious place would have been in the Crystal Palace, but its revised version at Sydenham was not ready and in any case their Crystal Palace, like our own, was the subject of bitter controversy, but for a very different reason. It had been suggested by Prince Albert, and Queen Victoria, at its inception, wrote to Lord John Russell, her Prime Minister, "The House of Commons is becoming very unmanageable and troublesome." Rankling in the royal bosom too was the British aristocracy's dislike of her adored Albert. This German princeling was so unpopular that vulgar music-hall doggerel was printed on broadsides, which caricatured the Prince Consort as "The German Lad was raving mad."

The bitterest attacks were in the Commons and the House of Lords where Albert's pet scheme for the "Great Exhibition" came up for discussion. He thought that something *must* be done to celebrate Britain's imperial splendor, her dominance of the sea, her extraordinary progress in manufactures—all the things that Germany lacked in 1848. His scheme was the notorious Crystal Palace, an iron and glass monstrosity covering acres and enclosing live trees in Hyde Park. The uproar at this suggestion weakened Albert's health, but he persisted with typical German pertinacity.

So virulent were the attacks that it was said in the Lords, for instance, that he had no right to set up the exhibition in Hyde Park. In the Commons it was suggested

The story of Sequoia

that it would attract all "the foreign rogues and revolutionists," subvert morals, steal trade secrets from England, even destroy the people's "faith and loyalty to their sovereign." The most troublesome of Albert's critics was a certain Col. Charles de Laet Waldo Sibthorp, a member from Lincoln. He warned that "secret societies were already being formed on the Continent to assassinate the Queen: worse still there would be an influx of papists, bringing with them idolatry, schism, bubonic plague, and venereal diseases. It was all too horrible to contemplate and all the doing of that damned German Prince."

Albert turned a deaf ear to these pleasantries and finally chose, from over two hundred designs, the one offered by Joseph Paxton, a man as remarkable in his way as the Prince Consort. Paxton was an architect, a gardener, and ultimately a statesman, and very proficient in all three. He had recently designed what was then the largest greenhouse in the world for the Duke of Devonshire at Chatsworth, and it was an extension of this idea which resulted in the Crystal Palace.

The exhibition opened on May 1, 1851, with a glittering galaxy of England's great, tens of thousands of "the common people," and exhibits from all over the world. This was balm to Prince Albert for the "Great Exhibition" was an enormous popular success, and actually cleared enough money to start what is now the Victoria and Albert Museum at South Kensington.

The Queen, naturally, was in ecstasy: here was a triumph for England, for her Empire, but most of all for her beloved husband, whose treatment by the Lords and Commons had been "most shabby." After a terrific day of excitement and adulation she confided to her much underlined *Journal*, "God bless my dearest Albert, God bless my dear-

The same specimen of Sequoia gigantea, *which had been shown in New York in 1855, went to London's Crystal Palace at Sydenham, and over twenty-seven thousand people saw it on the opening day, April 10, 1857. (Courtesy of Mr. Francis P. Farquhar, and permission to use this illustration from his* Yosemite, the Big Trees and the High Sierra, *University of California Press, 1948.)*

DESCRIPTION OF THE
MAMMOTH TREE FROM CALIFORNIA,
NOW ERECTED AT THE
CRYSTAL PALACE, SYDENHAM

1.—Whole Height of Tree . . 363 Feet
2.—Height to First Limb . . . 140 Feet
3.—Diameter at Base . . . . 31 Feet
4.—Diameter 100 Feet from the Base 15 Feet
5.—Bark at Base   18 Inches in Thickness
6.—Bark Removed to the Height of 116 Feet.

est country!" She even had a word for "Mr. Paxton, who might be justly proud and rose from being a common gardener's boy." There is no record that this bit of royal snobbery embarrassed her later when she was induced to make him Sir Joseph Paxton. He was then the editor of one of England's leading botanical magazines, an MP from Coventry, and a magnate in the growing railways.

In spite of the world-wide success of the exhibition there was still grumbling at its defacement of Hyde Park, and Paxton moved it bit by bit to Sydenham and much enlarged it. There it became a permanent exhibit room of gigantic proportions, but it was not ready when Trask landed in London in the fall of 1855.

Small and almost private showings of this huge tree were, however, possible in the spring of 1856. A section only sixteen feet high was shown in the Philharmonic Rooms in Oxford Street in the spring and in June it had been moved to the Adelaide Gallery in the Strand.

But such preliminary views of only small sections of *Sequoia gigantea* gave only a stunted version of the "vegetable monster." Actually, until the north transept of the Crystal Palace at Sydenham was completed, there was not a building in London where the whole exhibit could be staged. But the new Crystal Palace was finally opened to the public at one o'clock on Good Friday afternoon, April 10, 1857. Over twenty-seven thousand people went the first day, and as many more were turned away for lack of space. Its most gigantic single installation was, of course, the "vegetable monster from California," otherwise *Sequoia gigantea*, which had been brought over from New York by Mr. Trask.

The furor over the "vegetable monster" was hardly reflected in the admirably restrained catalog of the exhibits.

The story of Sequoia

With only a minimum of inaccuracy the official version reads:

> We are now standing at the foot of what represents one of the largest known trees in the world. This tree grew, one of a group of such monsters, on the Sierra Nevada in California. When flourishing it rose to the astonishing height of nearly 400 feet [actually it was "about 300 feet"]. Several in the same district, which are now standing are 300 feet in height. The bark of this tree has been arranged and fitted up as it grew, to give us some idea of its gigantic proportions by the view of the part. The wood is a particularly light cedar. Dr. Lindley has named it *Wellingtonia* [since changed to *Sequoia*] *gigantea,* and has fixed its age as 4,000 years.

The *Times* of London the next day had a news item reading:

> At the tropical end of the building, where the bark of the mammoth tree has been erected, there was, of course, a great crowd to pass upon that colossal specimen of Transatlantic vegetation. This tree, in comparison with which the great Adansonias of Cape Verde seem dwarfed to mere saplings, is from California, about 230 miles from San Francisco, and 15 from the diggings of Murphy's Camp.

There follows a repetition of then current tales about *Sequoia,* ending:

> . . . judging by its concentric rings botanists fix its age at 4000 years—an almost fabulous antiquity for a tree which was lately green and flourishing. According to this estimate it must have been growing when

[91]

THE AGELESS RELICTS

Nineveh was a mere collection of tents and ere the captive Jews began their labours on the Pyramids. The bark ... was cut from the tree in pieces eight feet long; each was marked and numbered, as it came off, so that the whole is now fastened together precisely as it stood for tens of centuries on the slopes of the Sierra Nevada. The thickness of the bark is 18 inches and the weight of the 90 feet erected at the Palace nearly 60 tons.

No wonder the British were stunned at this "Colossal specimen of Transatlantic vegetation," brought from its California home. The *Times* of April 15, 1857 carried a full column advertisement of the Crystal Palace, and it appears that they wanted to correct the dimensions given by the news item, which mentioned the height as 90 feet. The advertisement reads: "The portion erected in the Tropical Transept, opposite the Abu Simbel figures, is no less than 103 feet in height and 32 feet in diameter at the base."

There the only remaining exhibition of the earliest of these *Sequoia* trees was kept until the destruction of the Tropical Transept by fire in 1866.

Hundreds of thousands of people saw it in New York and London, most of whom would never see the living tree. Much of the literature put out about both exhibits was inaccurate, and some of it just plain exaggeration. But it is impossible to see these trees, either living in the Sierras or dead in the Crystal Palace, without a feeling that one has seen what many think is the eighth wonder of the world.

seven

WHAT'S IN A NAME?

EVER SINCE ITS DISCOVERY *Sequoia* has been plagued by pedants and patriots. When Lobb's specimens of the big-tree first reached England in 1853 the Duke of Wellington was the stout, somewhat profane, idol of the British public. Had he not won Waterloo and downed the Corsican tyrant? What more fitting than to christen the largest tree in the world in honor of England's greatest hero?

That is precisely what was done by Dr. Lindley, who proclaimed in print that he had christened the big-tree, in proper Latin, as *Wellingtonia gigantea*. Patriotism could scarcely crowd so much error into so few words, and Sir William Jackson Hooker, then director at the Royal Botanical Garden at Kew, scolded Dr. Lindley for not knowing that the big-tree already had a valid generic name and did not need a new one. The Lindley fiasco was published in 1853.

But California patriots were quick to resent this naming of their precious big-tree for any Englishman, even if he won the battle of Waterloo. Why not honor our greatest general, the Founder of our country, instead of this British idol. No sooner said than done. A certain Dr. C. F. Winslow, in the *California Farmer,* promptly, in 1854, christened the big-tree as *Washingtonia gigantea.* But Dr. Winslow was even more ignorant than Dr. Lindley.

Few things are so sacred to the experts as the priority of the Latin names of plants. Once a name is published and admitted to be valid, that name cannot be used for anything else. *Washingtonia,* however, apparently unknown to Winslow, is the perfectly valid name of a palm from southern California and, of course, quite incorrect for the big-tree.

Hence the professionals and the lay public were understandably a bit puzzled as to what was the correct name of the big-tree, not to speak of the redwood. The British mistake of 1853 and ours in 1854 appeared to leave the biggest tree in the world without a valid Latin name.

That such an unbaptized giant needed a correct name was so obvious that the experts soon began hunting for one. It then developed that neither England nor America was to have that honor, but a Hungarian. He was Stephan L. Endlicher of Vienna, who two years before he died, in 1849, published his *Synopsis Coniferarum.* There, on pages 197 and 198, he christened the redwood *Sequoia sempervirens.* This famous Vienna botanist thus established the generic name of *Sequoia,* and, according to all the rules, the *Wellingtonia gigantea* of Lindley and the *Washingtonia gigantea* of Winslow became *Sequoia gigantea,* which is

The story of Sequoia

still the only correct name for the big-tree, unless pedantry succeeds in supplanting it.

It is stated in all popular books about *Sequoia* and in many technical ones that Endlicher chose the generic name *Sequoia* to honor a half-breed Cherokee Indian who invented a Cherokee alphabet. This worthy took the name of George Guess, an American, because he believed him to be his father. His Indian name was Sequoya or Sequoyah, and he became famous because he taught many of his people to read and write their own language. Such an engaging figure was certainly worth honoring, but there is no evidence that Endlicher had ever heard of him and his name does not appear at his description of the genus *Sequoia*.

With both trees safely christened it seemed as if there could be no sequel. But some experts were never quite sure that the big-tree and the redwood could possibly be brother and sister: perhaps only slightly distant cousins. There are undeniable technical differences, well known to the experts, but most of them felt that the differences did not warrant changing the name of either tree, for they had been in general use ever since the middle of the nineteenth century.

But pedantry is just as common among botanists as in other scientists and in 1930 one of them magnified these differences to such a point that he created a new genus for the big-tree, calling it *Sequoiadendron giganteum*. Scarcely any one in California has taken much notice of this, perhaps thinking of the absurdity of having to call the greatest collection of big-trees Sequoiadendron National Park! But some technical books still prefer *Sequoiadendron* to *Sequoia* and they have reasonably valid scientific reasons for this, if you ignore their indifference to a century of usage and the inconvenience of the public.

[95]

The passion for changing the names of plants appears to be hard to eradicate. Many botanists have succumbed to the virus, and in California there is a well-defined and deplorable tendency to tinker with the common names of the big-tree and the redwood.

Their suggestion is that the redwood should be called the *coast* redwood, and the big-tree the *Sierra* redwood. Neither suggestion is adopted here, nor was it used by Peattie in his excellent *Natural History of Western Trees*. The proposed changes help no one, for who can ever mistake the redwood for the big-tree? Both the latter names have been in use for over a century, they are embalmed in practically all the huge literature of *Sequoia*, and it is hoped they will be as permanent as the trees.

It is quite true that other common names have been applied to both trees. Their disposition is shown below.

BIG-TREE = *Sequoia gigantea*.
    Called by some the Sierra Redwood, Giant Sequoia, Gigantea, Mammoth Tree, and California big-tree.

REDWOOD = *Sequoia sempervirens*.
    Called by some the Coast Redwood, California Redwood, Coastal Sequoia, Sempervirens, and Palo Colorado, the original Spanish name of the redwood. Another Spanish name for it was Palo Alto (tall tree), now quite appropriately the name of a thriving California city.

eight

WHERE THEY CAN BE FOUND

WHILE THIS IS in no sense a guidebook to *Sequoia*-land it may be convenient to know where to look for both trees. Only relatively large areas, all now under protection, are listed below, chosen for their beauty, accessibility, and for the fact that nowhere on earth can the visitor see such majestic trees.

The information has been culled from records of the California State Parks publications, from Save-the-Redwoods League, from the National Park Service, and from "The Status of *Sequoia gigantea* in the Sierra Nevada," which was a report to the Legislature of California in 1952. Other records used are from the California State Forest Service, the U.S. Forest Service, the University of California, and the California Division of Beaches and Parks.

THE AGELESS RELICTS

BIG-TREE
(*Sequoia gigantea*)

Of the seventy-two known groves of this forest giant the following twenty-two localities are the most outstanding. All of them have individual names, such as Mariposa Grove, etc., but in the list below the word *grove* is omitted. They are arranged in the approximate order of their occurrence from north to south. Unless of special importance all groves of less than one hundred acres are omitted. Some of these groves are in areas impossible to reach by car. Some need considerable walking, and a few are on horseback trails.

1. NORTH CALAVERAS. 62 acres. The original grove discovered by A. T. Dowd in 1852 while trailing a wounded grizzly. It is in Calaveras Big Tree State Park on State Highway 4, in Calaveras County.
2. SOUTH CALAVERAS. 415 acres. Five miles south of North Calaveras (No. 1) and long threatened with lumbering. It was purchased and given to the State by the late John D. Rockefeller, Jr.
3. YOSEMITE NATIONAL PARK. Total acreage 758 thousand. Established in 1890. There are three groves of giant trees:
    Tuolumne. 60 acres. At Big Oak Flat Road in Tuolumne County.
    Merced. 100 acres. At Coulterville Road, Mariposa County.
    Mariposa. 230 acres. East of Wawona, Mariposa County.
4. NELDER. 480 acres. In Sierra National Forest, five miles south of the Mariposa Grove (See No. 3) in Madera County.

The story of Sequoia

5. CONVERSE BASIN AND CONVERSE MOUNTAIN. 2800 acres. It is northwest of Kings River Highway, Fresno County.
6. INDIAN BASIN. 700 acres. South of Converse Basin (No. 5) on the Kings River Highway, Fresno County.
7. EVANS. 60 acres. East of Hume Lake, Fresno County.
8. WINDY GULCH. 2100 acres. East of Hume Lake, Fresno County.
9. KENNEDY. 200 acres. East of Hume Lake, Fresno County.
10. BIG STUMP. 640 acres. Partly on State Highway 180, in Kings Canyon National Park.
11. WHITAKER FOREST. 320 acres. Under management of the University of California, at Redwood Mountain, Fresno County. The best place to see controlled reproduction of the big-tree.
12. KINGS CANYON AND SEQUOIA NATIONAL PARKS. Total acreage over 800 thousand. Kings Canyon (established 1940) and Sequoia (established 1890), which adjoin each other, contain the greatest concentration of the big-tree. There are about 25 groves of which the following ten are the most important:

   General Grant. 510 acres. Kings Canyon National Park.

   Redwood Mountain. 3920 acres. Kings Canyon National Park.

   Muir. 300 acres. Sequoia National Park.

   Giant Forest. 2400 acres. Sequoia National Park. This is the place most visited by tourists because of ease of access, accommodations, parking facilities, etc. On the north end of the grove is "the biggest tree in the world," named for General Sherman. It is 273.9 feet high, 37.3 feet in diameter, and estimated as about thirty-five hundred years old.

THE AGELESS RELICTS

Many trees in this grove were given fanciful names, such as Burnt Twins, Black Chamber, Dead Giant, etc.; or named for such persons as Washington, Lincoln, Roosevelt, etc. Such designations add nothing to the majesty of the forest and seem a bit naïve to many.

Atwell Mill. 1320 acres. Sequoia National Park.
East Fork. 790 acres. Sequoia National Park.
Oriole Lake. 230 acres. Sequoia National Park.
Eden Creek. 900 acres. Sequoia National Park.
South Fork. 450 acres. Sequoia National Park.
Garfield. 2220 acres. Sequoia National Park.

13. MOUNTAIN HOME. 1700 acres, in Mountain Home State Forest, Tulare County. An additional 325 acres is in Sequoia National Forest, and 160 acres in Balch Park, Tulare County.
14. CRYSTAL SPRINGS. 320 acres, in Mountain Home State Forest in Tulare County.
15. WHEEL MEADOW. 610 acres in Sequoia National Forest on the East Fork of Tule River, Tulare County.
16. BLACK MOUNTAIN. 910 acres in Sequoia National Forest, at East Fork and South Fork of the Tule River divide, Tulare County.
17. FREEMAN CREEK. 520 acres in Sequoia National Forest in the Kern River drainage, Tulare County.
18. RED HILL. 310 acres in Sequoia National Forest, on the South Fork of Tule River, Tulare County.
19. PEYRONE. 340 acres in Sequoia National Forest, on the South Fork of Tule River, Tulare County.
20. PARKER PEAK. 640 acres on the Tule Indian Reservation, on the South Fork of Tule River, Tulare County.

The story of Sequoia

21. STARVATION CREEK. 200 acres in Sequoia National Forest in the Deer Creek drainage, Tulare County.
22. PACKSADDLE. 240 acres in Sequoia National Forest in the Deer Creek drainage, Tulare County.

REDWOOD
(*Sequoia sempervirens*)

While the original stand of redwood was well over one million acres, about half of which has been cut, the acreage preserved for posterity seems pitifully small. Somewhere about seventy thousand acres are in permanent preserves, largely because of the foresight of Save-the-Redwoods League and the State of California. Between them they have spent many millions of dollars to acquire the finest of redwood groves, especially in the northern part of the state where the preserved groves total over fifty thousand acres. Further south the preserved acreage is about four thousand, and in the Santa Cruz region over sixteen thousand acres.

The list of the finest groves includes only sizable, preserved tracts in California, but no private groves. The redwood peters out as one enters southern Oregon where there is only a small acreage, little of which is preserved. And in Oregon the redwood "is generally a minor species in Douglas fir stands," according to H. C. Obye, Forest Supervisor of Siskiyou National Forest.

The list below begins in the north, where the finest stands are found, and ends in the Santa Cruz region, near Monterey which, except for scattered trees, is the southern limit of the tree. All are near the coast or on it, and the finest groves are in the Coast Range of mountains, or in the valleys between them. The chief groves, all but one State Parks, are:

1. JEDEDIAH SMITH REDWOODS. 9539 acres. Six to nine miles northeast of Crescent City, near U.S. 199, on the Smith River, Del Norte County. In it is a tablet to Jedediah Smith, the Bible-Toter, who was an early explorer and discovered the river in 1828.
2. DEL NORTE COAST REDWOODS. 5852 acres. Eight miles south of Crescent City, on U.S. 101, Del Norte County. One of the largest groves close to the Pacific.
3. PRAIRIE CREEK REDWOODS. 9568 acres. Six miles north of Orick, on U.S. 101, Humboldt County. In this large preserve is the last surviving herd of the Roosevelt elk in California.
4. PATRICK'S POINT. 425 acres. Thirty miles north of Eureka, on U.S. 101, Humboldt County. A comparatively small grove close to the Pacific.
5. GRIZZLY CREEK REDWOODS. 149 acres. Thirty-five miles southeast of Eureka, on State Highway 36, Humboldt County.
6. HUMBOLDT REDWOODS. 23,462 acres. This is the most important of all the redwood preserves. It is all on or near the Avenue of the Giants Parkway or between it and the Pacific. It contains many individual and small memorial groves, all in Humboldt County. The main ones are:

Garden Club of America Grove.

Founders Grove. Named in honor of Henry Fairfield Osborn, Madison Grant, and J. C. Merriam, who founded Save-the-Redwoods League. The tallest known redwood, called the Founders Tree, occurs in this grove. It is reputedly 364 feet high.

The story of Sequoia

Rockefeller Redwood Forest, perhaps the finest of all redwood stands, comprising about 8000 acres, in the lower or northeastern part of the drainage of Bull Creek. It was purchased by the State with a gift of two million dollars by the late John D. Rockefeller, Jr.

Children's Forest.

The drive through these incomparable forests is one of the most impressive sights on earth. Nowhere is such grandeur so accessible, and for nearly 50 miles the effect is all but overpowering.

7. RICHARDSON GROVE. 751 acres. Nine miles south of Garberville, on U.S. 101, Humboldt County. A magnificent grove about 225 miles north of San Francisco.
8. STANDISH-HICKEY GROVE. 635 acres. Near the junction of U.S. 101 and the Shoreline Drive, in Leggett Valley, Mendocino County.
9. MONTGOMERY WOODS. 647 acres. Fifteen miles northwest of Ukiah, on U.S. 101, Mendocino County.
10. HENDY WOODS. 587 acres. Three miles west of Philo, on State Highway 128, Mendocino County.
11. MAILLIARD REDWOODS. 242 acres. Thirty miles southwest of Ukiah, on State Highway 128, Mendocino County.
12. ARMSTRONG REDWOODS. 440 acres. Twenty-three miles west of Santa Rosa, Sonoma County.
13. PETRIFIED FOREST. 585 acres. Fifteen miles east of Santa Rosa, Sonoma County. This is the most spectacular collection of fossilized redwood trunks, scattered among living trees.
14. BRANNON ISLAND. 224 acres. Three and one half miles south of Rio Vista, on State Highway 12, Sacramento County and probably the most easterly of all preserved redwood groves. It is about 70 miles east of the Pacific.

THE AGELESS RELICTS

15. MUIR WOODS. 485 acres. A National Monument, only 11 miles northwest of San Francisco, on the Shoreline Highway, Marin County.
16. PORTOLA. 1665 acres. Twenty miles west of Palo Alto, on Page Mill Road, San Mateo County.
17. BUTANO. 1955 acres. Seven miles southeast of Pescadero, and difficult of access, San Mateo County.
18. BIG BASIN REDWOODS. 11,033 acres. Twenty-three miles northwest of Santa Cruz, on State Highway 9, Santa Cruz County.
19. HENRY W. COWELL REDWOODS. 1737 acres. Seven miles northwest of Santa Cruz, on State Highway 9, Santa Cruz County.

It should be noted that in Numbers 16 to 19 inclusive, the trees do not compare in density, height, or girth with those north of San Francisco, probably because of insufficient rainfall.

BIBLIOGRAPHY

THE LITERATURE ON *Sequoia* comprises thousands of items, some of them technical, others fanciful and often inaccurate. Obviously it is impossible here to list even a fraction of the total. The abbreviated list below has been found useful and is suggested to those who may wish to explore features of the big-tree and redwood that it is impossible to include here.

Beyond the list below there are sources that should not be ignored. For instance, much information can be gleaned from the New York *Herald,* New York *Tribune,* New York *Times,* and from the *Evening Post* for the years 1853-56. Similarly the files of the *Times* of London, *Illustrated London News,* London *Morning Advertiser,* and *Gleason's Pictorial Drawing-room Companion* are rich in early *Sequoia* history. So is the *Gardeners' Chronicle* of London.

The list below also omits all technical reference books, all those on the culture of both trees in the East, and all specialized books on timber, lumber, bark, and utilization of the redwood. The much-winnowed list follows, together with some notes on their content.

ANONYMOUS. The Status of *Sequoia gigantea* in the Sierra Nevada. *Report to the California Legislature,* 1952. Sacramento.
> A detailed account of all public and the very few privately owned big-tree groves. Accurate and with complete statistics of location, acreage, etc.

ANONYMOUS. Big Trees of California. *Report of the Division of Forestry to the U.S. Department of Agriculture,* 1900. Washington.
> One of the earliest authoritative accounts of the big-tree and its threatened destruction at the beginning of the present century.

ANONYMOUS. *Mammoth Tree at the Crystal Palace* (London). Printed by R. S. Francis, Catherine Street. 1857. London.
> An account of the exhibit of the big-tree at the Crystal Palace, London.

ASBURY, HERBERT. *The Barbary Coast.* Pocket Books (Cardinal Edition). 1957. New York.
> A most readable account of San Francisco following the Gold Rush, the city's most lurid episode.

CLARK, GALEN. *The Big Trees of California.* Published by the author. 1907. Yosemite Valley, California.
> A popular account of the big-tree, as seen by one of the earlier observers.

CRAIG, HARMON. Carbon[13] Variations in *Sequoia* Rings and the Atmosphere. *Science,* January 29, 1954, pages 141-143. Washington.
> One of a long list of papers by the author and others, showing the response to moisture of the big-tree, often hundreds of years ago.

The story of Sequoia

DOUGLASS, A. E. *Climatic Cycles and Tree-Growth.* Carnegie Institution Publication No. 289. 1919. Washington.
>A correlation of climatic cycles and the growth of trees.

ELLSWORTH, R. S. *The Giant Sequoia.* Published by J. D. Berger. 1924. Oakland, California.
>A good popular account.

FARQUHAR, F. P. *Yosemite, the Big-Trees and the High Sierras.* A selective bibliography. University of California Press. 1948. Berkeley.
>By far the most scholarly account of all the early and now rare books on the big-tree and its environs.

FISHER, R. T. A Study of the Redwood. *Bureau of Forestry Bulletin No. 38.* 1903. Washington.
>One of the earliest authoritative accounts of the redwood forests, its timber potentialities and its threatened destruction early in this century.

FRITZ, EMANUEL. *California Coast Redwood.* An annotated bibliography. Foundation for American Resource Management. 1957. San Francisco.
>The most complete and accurate list of over 2000 titles on the redwood. The book is now distributed by the Forest History Society, St. Paul, Minnesota.

GRAY, ASA. *Sequoia and Its History. Address to the American Association for the Advancement of Science,* at Dubuque, Iowa. Salem Press. 1872. Salem, Massachusetts.
>The classic paper on *Sequoia* and its geological antiquity.

HUNTINGTON, ELLSWORTH. *Tree Growth and Climatic Interpretations.* Extracted from Carnegie Institution Publication 352. 1924. Washington.

A rather technical but thoroughly engrossing account of the effect of climate on tree growth.

HOLLINGSHEAD, JOHN. *Official Illustrated Guide to the Crystal Palace and Park.* 1866. London.

HUTCHINGS, J. M. *The Miners' Own Book.* Hutchings and Rosenfield. 1858. San Franciso.

> The best account of the conditions resulting from the Gold Rush of 1849. Contains the Miners' Ten Commandments, which, reprinted separately, sold thousands of copies.

HUTCHINGS, J. M. *In the Heart of the Sierras, Yo Semite Valley, the Big Trees.* Pacific Press Publishing House. 1886. Oakland, California.

> An extremely colorful miner who turned author and knew the big-tree almost from its discovery.

JACKSON, J. H. *Anybody's Gold.* D. Appleton—Century Co. 1941. New York.

> Gold mining in California.

KING, CLARENCE. *Mountaineering in the Sierra Nevada.* James R. Osgood & Co. 1875. Boston.

> A noted geologist and explorer who was in the Sierra Nevada in 1864 and much later was influential in founding the U.S. Geological Survey.

LEONARD, ZENAS. *Narrative of the Adventures of Zenas Leonard.* The Burrows Brothers Company. 1904. Cleveland.

> An account of the Walker expedition of 1833. It was on this trip through the Sierras that Leonard found the big-tree, and he was almost certainly the first white man ever to see it. His book was originally published at Clearfield, Pa., but was largely lost until reprinted early in this century.

The story of Sequoia

MUIR, JOHN. *The Mountains of California*. Century Co. 1894. New York.
>Perhaps the best-loved, most sensitive amateur naturalist who ever wrote about the Sierras.

PEATTIE, D. C. *A Natural History of Western Trees*. Houghton Mifflin Co. 1953. Boston.
>The best tree book for the general reader on the trees native from the Rocky Mountains to the Pacific.

REVEAL, JACK, and WALLEN, ARNOLD. *The Redwood Forest Handbook*. California State Board of Forestry. 1952. Sacramento.

SCHULMAN, EDMUND. Tree-Ring Hydrology in Southern California. *Laboratory of Tree-Ring Research Bulletin No. 4*. University of Arizona. 1947. Tucson.
>Dr. Schulman has convinced most scientists that certain pine trees may be older than the big-tree.

ST. BARBE BAKER, RICHARD. *The Redwoods*. George Ronald. 1959. London.
>A modern, popular account of the main preserved groves by an enthusiastic and perceptive writer.

STRACHEY, LYTTON. *Queen Victoria*. Harcourt, Brace & Co. 1921. New York.
>Toward the end of the fourth chapter is an account of how the London Crystal Palace was initiated by Prince Albert, and the opposition to it.

WOOD, R. C. *Murphy's, Queen of the Sierras. A History of Murphy's Camp*. Calaveras Californian. 1948. Angel's Camp, California.
>A history of Murphy's Camp from which A. T. Dowd went to Calaveras and "discovered" the big-tree in 1852, for no one then knew of the Leonard discovery in 1833.

INDEX

Containing the names of people, plants and places, except those in chapter eight and the bibliography.

Adams, Alvin, 78, 85
Alaska, 50
Albert, Prince, 86-87
American Association for the Advancement of Science, 38
American Museum of Curios, 75
American River, 3
Avenue of the Giants Parkway, 66
Ayala, Don Manuel, 58

B

Barbary Coast, 17
Barnum, P. T., 75, 77
Beecher, H. W., 11, 77
Bennett, James Gordon, 74, 82

Bernard of Clairvaux, 37, 54
bibliography, 105-109
Bidwell, John, 9
big-tree
  age, 26
  antiquity, 37-45
  associated trees, 28
  cones and needles, 14
  discovery, 9-10
  distribution, 10-11, 28
  exhibits
    San Francisco, 17-21
    New York, 74-86
    London, 86-92
  geological history, 37-45
  introduction into England, 17
  nomenclature, 93-96
  reproduction, 29-31

INDEX

big-tree (*cont'd.*)
    size and weight, 26-27
big-tree preserved groves, 98-101
Bodega Bay, 60
Boston, 21
Bryant Park, 75
burls, 68

C

Cabrillo, J. R., 55
Calaveras County, 5, 6
Calaveras Grove, 10, 12, 16, 29
California big-tree, 96
California Farmer, 94
California Redwood, 96
Cherokee Indian, 95
Chicago, 21
Clark Dodge & Co., 37
Clearfield, Pa., 9
Coastal Sequoia, 96
Coast Range, 72
Coast Redwood, 96
Cobbe, Frances P., 41
Coloma, 3
cone-scales, 45
Costanso, Miguel, 59
Cretaceous, 44
Crespi, Fray Juan, 58
crocodile, 42
Croton Reservoir, 75
Crystal Palace
    New York, 75-86
    London, 87-92

D

Darwinism and Morals, 41

"dawn redwood," 49
Del Norte County, 72, 102
Donetti's Acting Monkeys, 76
Douglas squirrel, 25
Dowd, A. T., 5, 8
Drake, Sir Francis, 58
Drake's Bay, 58
Dubuque, Iowa, 37
Duke of Devonshire, 87
Duke of Sutherland, 11
Duke of Wellington, 93

E

El Cabo de Pinos, 55
Endlicher, S. L., 94
England, 17, 41
Eucalyptus, 66

F

Farquhar, F. P., 88
Fillmore, President, 77
fire, 22, 29, 30
fog, 69
Fort Ross, 55, 60
fossil *Sequoia,* 42-50
Founders Tree, 102
Fritz, Emanuel, 61

G

Gardeners' Chronicle, 12
Garfield, President, 11
General Sherman tree, 99
Giant Forest, 46, 99
Giant Sequoia, 96
Gigantea, 96

INDEX

ginkgo, 42, 45
Gleason's Pictorial, 12
Golden Gate Bridge, 27
gold rush, 3-8
Gordon-Cummings, C. F., 20
Grant, Madison, 63
Gray, Asa, 11, 39, 53
Greeley, Horace, 11, 74, 82
Greenland, 50
groves, protected
   big-tree, 98-101
   redwood, 101-104
Guess, George, 95

H

Hall of Fame, 53
Hanford, Captain, W. H., 80
Homer, 26
Hooker, Sir William J., 93
Humboldt County, 70, 72, 102, 103
Hutchings, J. M., 8, 16
Hyde Park, 86

I

ice sheet, 49
Illustrated London News, 12, 17
incense cedar, 28
Ingersoll, Robert, 42

J

Jenny Lind, 75

K

Kent, Mr. & Mrs. William, 66

Kew, 93
Kings Canyon National Park, 11, 31, 99

L

Lake Tahoe, 11
Leonard, Zenas, 9
Lindley, John, 93
"living fossil," 49, 55
Lobb, William, 17, 93

M

Mammoth Tree, 96
Mammoth Tree Grove, 6
Marin County, 58, 60
Mariposa Grove, 10, 18, 29, 32, 98
Marshall, John, 3
Mendocino County, 72, 103
Merced County, 98
Merriam, J. C., 63
Metasequoia, 48, 49
Metropolitan Hotel (New York), 78
Mexico, 60
Monterey, 52, 58, 69
"Mother of the Forest," 20, 83, 85
Muir, John, 24, 27
Muir Woods, 58, 64, 66, 104
Murphy's Camp, 4-11, 83, 91

N

Natural History of Western Trees, 69, 96

[*113*]

INDEX

New Spain, 58
New York *Evening Express,* 84
New York *Evening Post,* 84
New York *Herald,* 74, 77, 78, 79, 82
New York Public Library, 75
New York *Times,* 75, 77, 79, 82
New York *Tribune,* 3, 74, 83
New Yorker, The, 74
Niblo's Gardens, 76
North Calaveras Grove, 9, 98

O

Oregon, 52, 55, 69, 72
Osborn, Henry Fairfield, 63
ovule, 45

P

"pail of protoplasm," 42
Pajaro River, 58
Palo Alto, 96
Palo Colorado, 96
Paris, 21
Paxton, Joseph, 87, 90
Peattie, Donald Culross, 69, 96
Petrified Forest, 44, 103
Philadelphia, 21
Pinchot, Gifford, 63
pollen, 45
Portola expedition, 58
Portuguese navigators, 55
Prairie Creek Redwoods, 70, 102
preserved groves
  big-tree, 98-101
  redwood, 101-104
New Albion, 58

Q

Quarternary, 44
Quirk, William, 9

R

Racket Court, 78
rainfall, 69, 104
Record, S. J., 61
red fir, 28
redwood
  area of original forest, 61-62
  burls, 68
  cones and needles, 56, 67
  discovery, 58-59
  exploitation, 61
  influence of fog, 69
  lumbering, 61-63
  reproduction, 62, 67-68
  Russian lumbering, 60
  Save-the-Redwoods League, 63-66
  size and girth, 6
  value of lumber, 59, 61-62
redwood coffin, 59
Redwood Highway, 63
redwood preserved groves, 101-104
Richardson Grove, 66, 103
Rockefeller, John D., Jr., 9, 34, 98, 103
Roosevelt, Theodore, 63, 66
Royal Botanical Garden, 93
Russian lumbering, 60
Russian River, 60

INDEX

S

San Francisco, 4, 16, 17, 58, 104
San Joaquin Valley, 51
Santa Rosa, 44
Save-the-Redwoods League, 63, 66, 101
Scudder's American Museum, 75
Sempervirens, 96
Sequoia
  gigantea. see big-tree
  sempervirens. see redwood
Sequoia and its History, 40-54
Sequoia National Park, 11, 31, 99
Sequoiadendron giganteum, 95
Sequoya or Sequoyah, 95
Serra, Junipero, 59
Siberia, 50
Sibthorp, C. de L. W., 87
Sierra Nevada, 11, 25-36
Sierra redwood, 96
silver fir, 24
Sixth Avenue Railway, 77
Smith, A. J., 32
Smith's Cabin, 32
Sonoma County, 44, 72, 103
Sonora *Herald*, 9
South Calaveras Grove, 34, 98
Spanish navigators, 55
Spitzbergen, 50
Stanislaus River, 8
sugar pine, 28
Sutters Mill, 3
Swedish Nightingale, 75
Sydenham, 90
Sydney Ducks, 17

T

Tertiary, 44
Timbers of the New World, 61
Times of London, 76
Tom Thumb, 75
Tuolumne County, 34, 98
Trask, G. D., 20, 85, 90
Tree Mastodon, 83
Trinity Corners, 46
Tulare County, 31, 100
tunnel tree, 32

U

Uncle Tom's Cabin, 76
U.S. Forest Service, 63
University of California, 31, 99

V

Veitch & Son, 17
Victoria, Queen, 86-88
Victoria and Albert Museum, 87
Viscaino expedition, 58

W

Walker, F. R., 9
Washingtonia gigantea, 83, 94
Watsonville, 58
Wellingtonia gigantea, 91, 93
Whitaker Forest, 31, 99
white-barked pine, 28
white fir, 28
Winslow, C. F., 94
Wooster, J. M., 9

Y

yellow pine, 28
Yerba Buena, 3